"Would you like to smell my prickmadam?"

(That's one horticulturist speaking to another.)

If an old aunt offers you a boat ride up the *River Suck* in Ireland, if your stockbroker calls to ask you about *cum rights*, or if your boss sends you a memo on *loose coupling, direct coupling,* and *self-excitation*, should you respond with aplomb or with a gasp?

Don't be left embarrassed when you are introduced to a *chick sexer* at a party. You'll be able to keep your cool because you've got the book that tells all about terms that sound taboo but are completely acceptable in polite society.

DAVID GRAMBS is a lexicographer, translator, and author whose books include *Dimboxes, Epopts, and Other Quidams; The Ultimate Spelling Quiz Book;* and *The Describer's Dictionary.* He was an editor of the second edition of the unabridged *Random House Dictionary,* as well as several other reference works. He lives in New York City.

David Grambs

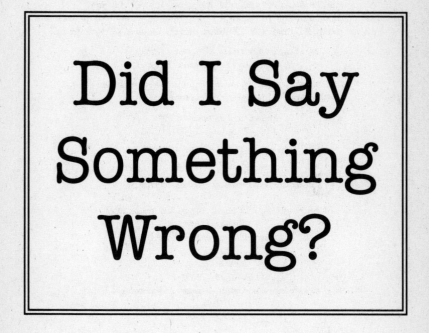

Did I Say Something Wrong?

Illustrated by Mary Kornblum

A PLUME BOOK
FOR WORD WATCHERS

PLUME

Published by the Penguin Group
Penguin Books USA Inc., 375 Hudson Street, New York, New York 10014, U.S.A.
Penguin Books Ltd, 27 Wrights Lane, London W8 5TZ, England
Penguin Books Australia Ltd, Ringwood, Victoria, Australia
Penguin Books Canada Ltd, 10 Alcorn Avenue, Toronto, Ontario, Canada M4V 3B2
Penguin Books (N.Z.) Ltd, 182–190 Wairau Road, Auckland 10, New Zealand

Penguin Books Ltd, Registered Offices:
Harmondsworth, Middlesex, England

First published by Plume, an imprint of New American
Library, a division of Penguin Books USA Inc.

First Printing, January, 1993
3 5 7 9 10 8 6 4 2

 REGISTERED TRADEMARK—MARCA REGISTRADA

Library of Congress Cataloging-in-Publication Data
Grambs, David.
Did I say something wrong? / David Grambs.
p. cm.
Includes index.
ISBN 0-452-26831-1
1. English language—Semantics—Humor. 2. Vocabulary—Humor.
I. Title.
PE1574.G75 1993
422'.0207—dc20   92-18998
                                                        CIP
Printed in the United States of America
Set in American Typewriter and Times Roman

Designed by Steven N. Stathakis

To Ellen

Contents

Acknowledgments

For their personal aid and comfort, I'm indebted to Reinhold Aman, Laurence Davies, Diane Giddis, Ian Jackman, Frank Lyman, Luther Miller, Rick Pearse, and Roy West. I'd also like to thank my editor, Rachel Klayman, and, for not charging me any rent, the New York Public Library and Baker Library at Dartmouth College.

Publisher's Warning:

Reading all or parts of this book aloud may be socially hazardous.

Did I Say Something Wrong?

Preface

This is a shockingly clean book. As its reassuring glossaries show, there is not a single objectionable word in its pages. Of course, as human beings, we're all rather suggestible, and there's no accounting for the dirty minds of some people.

But there will doubtless be a reader or two who will remark that this little tome is having fun at the expense of the English language.

Well, turnabout is fair play. If you aren't particularly aware of it now, maybe this book will remind you that our English language has always had its own great fun at our expense. It knows how to make its struggling users nervous and causes us to shy away from certain perfectly innocent words. Or, more accurately, we could call them not-guilty words. The lexicon of English has more of these words than you might think. Consciously or unconsciously, we've all been practicing safe lex since we were born.

Many words in our national tongue have upstanding meanings but sure don't look or sound that way to healthy, red-eared Americans. Expressions like functor, nympholept, cuirass, double-tonguing, penistone, and bra cheese. Because these unfamiliar words resemble familiar dirty or "delicate" words, they make people uncomfortable and put straight faces at risk.

This is a most interesting, smirky twilight zone of English. Yet who has ventured there for an unflinching look around?

We shouldn't have to spend our social lives anxiously avoiding such terms as (are you still a mite uncomfortable from those mentioned above?) tittup, bissextile, quincunx, exsuccous, homeopath, intestate, mastication, penetralia, crapulous, fartlek, coccyx, and climax basket. Or be nervous about even more innocent words in certain contexts. Why is it we feel fine asking for a lubricant from a garage or gas station worker but not from a young salesgirl in a pharmacy?

In certain situations, words must be chosen with particular

care. Would you tell a notoriously adulterous politician that you don't mean to interfere in his affairs? Inquire of a reportedly rich man if he indeed has piles? Ask the owner of an old hatchback if he'd be interested in a cheap pickup? Compliment a female biker on her cycle? Tell a butcher whom you appreciate that nobody can beat his meat? Ask your driver in the desert if she will soon be passing water? Question an ailing bride just back from the honeymoon as to whether she feels over the hump yet?

Should something called a "petting zoo" be any place to take children? Is a "pupu platter" any kind of a name for food? If you were a perfectly clean comb or hairbrush, would you want to be referred to as a member of the "toilet set"?

Of course, you can always avoid close-call words and expressions by using different words with the same meaning. Well, most of the time, but not always. For instance, in the realm of engineering and tools there's a kind of metal collar used to connect the ends of shafts called a muff coupling. In polite society who wants to talk about muff couplings? Time to practice safe lex. Time for a synonym. You look it up. The synonym is box coupling, and reading further, you find out that there are two kinds, the lap box coupling and the butt box coupling. Is this any improvement?

Can we turn to our greatest literature for safer lex?

Take, for example, this innocent sentence from James Fenimore Cooper's *The Pioneers:*

The door was unfastened, and Richard entered with the freedom that characterized not only the intercourse between the cousins, but the ordinary manners of the Sheriff.

Would you read it aloud to your average, sniggering American high school class?

Or how about this, from Rudyard Kipling's *Kim:*

For the rest—Kim giggled here as he cleaned his teeth—his hostess would rather heighten the enjoyment of the road. He inspected her bullocks critically, as they came up grunting and blowing under the yoke.

Have you ever inspected a woman's (or a man's) bullocks

critically? All right, maybe you have. But when they were grunting and blowing?

So, what about these curiously unnerving, taboo-seeming nouns, adjectives, verbs, and phrases that the English language is farctate (that's stuffed) with, that just have the misfortune to have been born as double entendres? Can't somebody finally give the black sheep of our native language their due?

Did I Say Something Wrong? is intended to do just that. Again, this is a shockingly clean book. Okay, cleanly shocking, if you insist. If the following pages seem like strong fare to you, just remember: They are indeed *like* strong fare, and it's all in your mind (all right, it was in my mind, too). The whole book—it's all just a big misunderstanding. Most sections are followed by glossaries. If part of the text is getting you a little hot under the collar, just turn for semantic relief to the glossary that follows it. (Many definitions, by the way, are simplified. Not intended to be rigorously technical or even complete, they are provided for only one purpose: to reassure.)

A word about pronunciations, which are not provided in these pages. Some of the terms in the book, it could be argued, have pronunciations that are unusual or slightly different from what they "look like" or from what would sound most suggestive. But the point here is that pronunciation is always a matter of hesitation where unfamiliar words are concerned. Not knowing, many basically circumspect people, a little uneasy, will at all costs avoid certain pronunciations. Now, why would they do that? This very uncertainty, this leeriness about leering words, makes all these too-close-for-comfort English words fair game.

No doubt about it, it's old Mother English who's having the fun, with us. But in the following pages we've taken quite a few of her underclothes, thrown them together unwashed (except for some bluing) into the machine, and hit that spin-cycle button. Here's hoping they don't emerge too hot to handle.

"I've always admired
Annie's gorgeous pumpkins."

Smutty Talk

Stunt, wilt, yellows, if not pecky dry rot—as if the economy weren't hard enough on agriculture, farmers have also been bothered recently by nagging diseases of their various crops and animals.

This was made all too clear in a recent telephone conversation between farmers Enos Brown and Betty Smith, soil-tilling and livestock-rearing neighbors in the American heartland.

After some initial talk about an exciting pickup contest and some shock rows, Enos got down to problems.

■   ■   ■

"I hope that bastard strangles—"

"Pardon, Enos?"

"I say, I hope that case of bastard strangles in your mare got taken care of by the vet."

"Sure 'nough," Betty said. "Everything's fine with Nellie in my horse house, except for some clap and horny slough, though Dobbin's got broken wind and a tender horny frog."

"Glad to hear it. Both my old nag and my favorite filly are cock-throppled."

"But, to make a clean breast of it, Enos, my milk production is utterly down. You want cream in your pints, you know. No Bang's disease, but got Texas itch and a bit of licking disease. I'm looking for gross abnormalities and have a couple of hired hands watching my strip cups—it's a hand's job. Also need some new balling forceps and a cream screw. How's that old bitch of yours?"

"She's got brown mouth. They say it's a virus, but I'm watching what she eats."

"At least we don't have all the problems with fruits the orchard people down the road are having," Betty said. "My cousin in Florida is always looking for the magnum bonum, but he has greasy spot and spreading decline, and fig smut, too. You know Annie Toony's nice pumpkins?"

"I've always admired Annie's gorgeous pumpkins," Enos said quickly. Annie, in turn, had been to Enos's barn and gone crazy over his equipment.

"Well, now her pumpkins have got curly top, and she's also got wet feet and standard prune constricting mosaic."

"Sad to hear," sympathized Enos, who knew poor Annie to be quite a sturdy hoer. "How's her sour cherry?"

"Western x-disease, I hear," said Betty. "My Billy—what a goat!—he just got over some sore mouth. But it's all my cereal crops, veggies and fruits, that's ailing."

"You're talking smut? Stinking smut?" Enos asked.

"You got it. I had an agriculture expert over here with lots of, you know, kernel knowledge. He knows kernel smut and head smut. Has written some book all about some stage of botrytis, something called *Botryotinia fuckeliana*. According to him, I'm up to my grasses in naked smut and nuda loose smut. And my stripping machine needs servicing. Take a healthy shallot, take your common leek—all this fungal sporing costs me money. My sizable bulbs are rotting. I've got yellow Bermudas, you know, and from the looks of it I've got moldy nose. How are your corn problems?"

"Might as well be back in the old bangboard days," Enos said. "My Indian's got boil smut," he said, "and head smut is eating up my corn whole. 'Course, you've always got to worry about frenching. A couple of years ago, I had Stewart's wilt and tipburn. I tell you, Betty, it's a fungused-up world for us farmers. Even an old farmhouse front-yard tree ain't safe. My cucumber's got mildew, and I've got butt rott. It's a real trunk murderer."

"Least we're not growing rice or tobacco," Betty philosophized. "Then we'd have to worry about false smut, or either black shank, pole rot, or wet butt."

"How're your little taters, Betty?"

"They've still got pock scab."

"Your fruits and drupes have problems, too?"

"I've got little cherry—half the normal size and bright red beyond picking time. You remember last year I had to worry about sweet cherry deep suture, bottom rot, and shot hole?"

"You don't say," Enos said.

"Maybe I'll go south and take up those big, healthy bananas, Enos."

"Then you'll have to worry about blackhead disease or bunchy top. An old horny-handed farmboy friend of mine went to the West Indies. Now his sugarcane's rotting from pokkah boeng, and he's got problems with his defecator."

"How do you like them apples."

"Please don't use that word," Enos sighed. "I have a taste for Rome Beauties, but damned if a lot of them turn out to be not so good after they're in the sack."

"You don't say."

"And while you've got little cherry, Betty, I've got cherry scab. Ever seen a freckled twig? Not to mention my swollen plums."

"You still got pocket plums?"

"I do, and beet pocket rot, too. Just can't get a handle on the problem. But these days I'm also spending lots of time in the henhouse."

"What's up there?"

"I've got blackhead and crazy chick disease. Got a lot of barebacks and breast blisters. I'm trying to increase vitamin E to all my chicks. The English fellow I just hired as a farmhand tells me my cock's not in such good shape, either, and I'm slowly going broke. By chance you be interested in an old but reliable gang-plow, Betty?"

GLOSSARY

balling forceps tongs used for giving pills to animals
bangboard an extra sideboard on a corn wagon for husks to be bounced off into the wagon
Bang's disease brucellosis
bareback a chicken with scant feathers on its back
bastard strangles a disease of horses
beet pocket rot a disease of beets
bitch a female dog
blackhead a disease of poultry
blackhead disease a disease of bananas
black shank a disease of tobacco
boil smut a disease of Indian corn
Botryotinia fuckeliana a certain stage of a rotting disease of apples, grapes, celery, and potatoes
botrytis a fungal imperfection causing plant diseases
bottom rot a disease of cabbage and lettuce
breast blister a keel cyst, or cystlike formation afflicting chickens and turkeys
broken wind a disease of old horses
brown mouth a disease of dogs
bunchy top a disease of bananas and other plants
butt rot a disease of trees
cherry scab a disease of cherries
clap a disease of horses
cock a rooster
cock-throppled (of horses) having a curved or bent windpipe
crazy chick disease a disease of young chickens
cream screw an orifice type of set screw on a cream separator
cucumber mildew a disease of cucumbers and melons
curly top a disease of beans and pumpkins
defecator a tank for purifying sugarcane juice
false smut green smut, a disease of rice
fig smut a disease of figs

filly   a young female horse

frenching   a disease of crops, especially of corn, cotton, and tobacco

fungal sporing   the producing of reproductive bodies by fungi

gangplow   a kind of double plow that can turn parallel furrows

greasy spot   a disease of citrus trees

head smut   a disease of corn and sorghum

horny frog   the foot pad of a horse

horny-handed   having callused hands

horny slough   sitback, a saddle-caused callosity on a horse's
back

kernel smut   covered smut, a disease of grains

licking disease   pica, a disease of cattle (also called licking sick-
ness)

little cherry   a disease of sweet cherries

magnum bonum   the largest or best variety of a fruit

moldy nose   a disease of onions, garlic, or shallots

nag   a worn-out old horse

naked smut   loose smut, a disease of plants, especially of cereal
grasses

nuda loose smut   a disease of barley

pickup contest   a butter-grading competition

pocket plum (or **plum pocket**)   a disease of plums

pock scab   powdery scab, a disease of potatoes

pokkah boeng (or **pokkah-bong**)   a disease of sugarcane

pole rot   pole sweat, a disease of tobacco (also called poleburn)

Rome Beauty   a type of apple

shallot   an onionlike perennial herb

shock row   a row of shocks (piles of hay)

shot hole   a disease of cherries

smut   any of various diseases mostly of cereal grasses

sore mouth   a disease of sheep and goats

sour cherry   a small tree with edible fruit

spreading decline   a disease of citrus fruit

standard prune constricting mosaic   a disease of prunes

Stewart's wilt a disease of corn

stinking smut bunt of wheat, a disease of wheat (also called high smut, low smut, pepper brand, and smut ball)

strip cup a metal cup for examining a cow's foremilk (or first-drawn milk)

stripping machine a harvesting machine that separates seed from standing grass

sweet cherry deep suture a disease of sweet cherries

swollen plums a disease of plums

Texas itch a form of cattle mange or scabies that forms in winter

tipburn a disease of lettuce

western x-disease a disease of peaches and sour cherries

wet butt a softening and discoloring of tobacco caused by premature freezing

wet feet a disease of raspberries

yellow Bermuda a type of onion

■   ■   ■   ■   ■   ■   ■   ■   ■

SCOTLAND, WALES, AND IRELAND TOUR!

A four-week guided tour-a-lure-a through Britain without the stiff upper lip. Learn a different kind of English! You will visit:

Tongue, Altass, Cock Bridge, Gartocharn, Bridge of Orchy, Beattock, Butt of Lewis, Bitch Burn, Cock, Assloss, Douchlage, Hairy Hillock, Dick's Law, Maiden Hair, Head-dykes, Peterhead, and Little Cocklick in Scotland

Little Cwm, Coity Pond, The Bitches, Penisarcwm, Bangor-is-y-coed, Pontypool Pantygasseg, and Offa's Dyke in Wales

Cummeenduff Glen, Holeopen Bay West, Laytown, and the River Suck in Ireland

FOR DETAILS AND BOOKINGS, CONTACT GLOBE-TROTS TRAVEL AGENCY

■   ■   ■   ■   ■   ■   ■   ■   ■

WHAT KIND OF TALK IS THAT? QUIZ NO. 1
In what subject or field are the following terms
used?

crazing   overflush
frigger   slop peck
Kelly ball test   suck-and-blow process
dirty finish   Manson effect
jiggering   cuckhold
junior cones   cupping

Answer on page 228.

Soon Steve claimed he was well-enaowed, asked to see my briefs, and made a plea for my bare trust.

Street Talk

Mary Lou, who works for an imposing financial firm, recently received the following letter from a close female friend, Wanda Meade, who has a law degree and works in a very conservative, high-pressure brokerage on Wall Street. The lingo of Wall Street is sometimes called Street talk. (A pin-striped wag suggested that the letter might easily be titled "My First and Last Gross Adventure.")

To those of us who know nothing of high finance and legal jargon, Wanda's letter doesn't make much sense. It seems, from all the terminology it is packed with, to be about a recent confusing financial or legal transaction with a male client named Steve.

But then again, maybe not. Wanda is evidently closely watched at work and has been known to write letters in a kind of legal-financial code language.

The publication of her letter, we've been assured, will have no adverse effect on the stock market.

■　■　■

Dear Mary Lou,

Regarding the new client, Steve, I mentioned to you on the phone last week (I am not writing naked here, if you get my drift), I've decided that they all want the same thing. Call it first in, first out.

I was in the market, to be sure, even though I certainly knew Steve looks on me as so many offer curves.

At the bar Friday evening, Steve again brought up the matter of a FOK order and complimented me on the glamour issue and on my being classy. He said he wanted some class action, and when I jokingly told him I was the law, he said he couldn't wait to take the law into his own hands. I could see he wanted to cop something, and it wasn't a plea.

I thought this was all about an extended bond, but Steve then mentioned a certain Christmas party.

Christmas party? Let's call it the Slutsky-Yule effect.

It was a gross adventure, with damaged goods everywhere and every member firm. And talk about insider trading! I regarded it all, as they coupled with interest, as damnum infectum and could only think ad rectum. There seemed to be no prophylactic rules, but I saw at least one affirmative pregnant. I never saw so many naked positions, ascending tops, and descending tops, and there was plenty of bottomry, and watching briefs too!

With so many naked options, I couldn't help wondering if there were position limits and exactly how many active boxes there were. I don't think any of the men present were intestate. Steve watched the rising bottoms and backend performance and hands-on management—there was little asset coverage—with such interest that I began to worry about his ticker. There was a certain assumption of skill and some backup withholding. Somebody would just roll forward, or reverse a swap, or split. I know some of them were married puts and common-law cheats, others just naked possessors. As for the hostess, I don't think she had any kind of dikephobia.

At one point Steve wanted me to lend him an ear, as his

tongue ventured forth. Did he think I was some kind of Q-tip trust? You know very well how, if you don't get the proper allowances, you're soon involved in fell agio.

Soon Steve claimed he was well-endowed, asked to see my briefs, and made a plea for my bare trust. He wanted a nude pact, for me to lift a leg while he held onto a bracket. I realized he was a bracket creep and had no interest in his attachment execution. Does everybody have cum rights? He told me I was eminently fungible, and I told him I had no use for an attractive nuisance.

What with all the tip-offs about insider trading and even the messiness of uncontrollable defalcation, the authorities finally came. Somebody fingered the hostess, but wouldn't you know somebody else got her off.

Your loving friend,
Wanda

GLOSSARY

active box   available collateral for customers' margin positions or brokers' loans (in the place where securities are kept)

ad rectum   to right or to do right (with respect to meeting an accusation or the law's demands)

affirmative pregnant   in law, an affirmative statement containing an implied negative that is favorable to the opposing party

agio   a currency-exchange premium or allowance

ascending tops   a chart pattern that shows over a period of time a security's price, with each price peak successively higher

asset coverage   the extent to which a debt, preferred stock class, etc., are covered by a company's net assets

assumption of skill   a doctrine pertaining to a master and the safety of a piece of work

attachment execution   in some states, a process of garnishment in order to satisfy a judgment

attractive nuisance a doctrine of tort law relating to property that creates potential dangers for children

backend performance in marketing, the buying and paying patterns of a customer in a relationship with a seller

backup withholding a particular 20 percent withholding tax on dividends and interest when the appropriate records have not been filed

bare trust a trust in which the trustee only holds title for the beneficiary

bottomry a type of mortgagelike contract in shipping

bracket creep a wage-earner's gradual moving into a higher federal income-tax bracket

brief a statement or memorandum of the salient points of a legal case

bulge a quick temporary rise in price affecting all of a stock or commodities market, or affecting one particular stock or commodity

class action a general legal action taken by more than one plaintiff when they have a common grievance

common-law cheat obtaining money or property by false means

coupled with interest referring, in the law of agency, to a written grant to the agent of an interest in the estate or property in question (as opposed to proceeds from exercising the agency)

cum rights with rights (said of certain stocks)

damaged goods shipped goods damaged during the voyage or while bonded in the warehouse

damnum infectum loss or damage that is anticipated but that hasn't yet occurred

defalcation embezzlement

descending tops a chart pattern showing that over time each new high price for a security is lower than the one preceding

dikephobia fear of justice

extended bond a matured bond on which the principal has not yet been paid

first in, first out (FIFO) an accounting for inventory by assuming that the inventory is sold in the same order in which it was bought

FOK order   a fill-or-kill order: to buy or sell a particular security whose cancellation is impending

fungible   interchangeable (in an obligation)

glamour issue   a very attractive and popular stock that keeps rising in price

gross adventure   loan of money upon bottomry

hands-on management   management closely involved in daily operations

insider trading   illegal use of privileged information in the buying and selling of securities

intestate   not having made a valid will

lift a leg   to close one side of a hedged transaction, leaving the other as a long or short position

married put   an option to sell a particular number of securities at a certain price by a specified time

member firm   a brokerage firm having a membership (at least one) on a major stock exchange despite the fact that the membership is in the name of an employee

naked option   a short position wherein the writer of the stock option has no hedging position in the security

naked position   a securities position that isn't hedged from market risk

naked possessor   a possessor of land without title or color of title (apparent but invalid title)

nude pact   an agreement not enforceable because of a lack of certain legal essentials

offer curve   a price-consumption curve

position limits   ceilings, determined by the SEC, on the number of option contracts a trader may control

prophylactic rules   a court's legal rules and customs to safeguard the truth, such as the oath and the penalty for perjury

Q-tip trust   (Qualified Terminable Interest Property Trust) a trust permitting assets to be transferred between spouses

reverse a swap   to restore a bond portfolio to a previous position after swapping one bond for another

rising bottom   a chart pattern that shows a rising trend in a low-priced commodity or security

roll forward   to move from one option position to another having a later date of expiration

Slutsky-Yule effect   in statistics and probability, cyclical (business) behavior in a time series caused by the very act of summing or determining average successive values of a random series

split   dividing of stock into more shares for existing shareholders

ticker   a telegraphic instrument that prints stock market quotations on paper tape

watching brief   a lawyer's retainer to observe proceedings at the behest of a person not a party to the proceedings

well-endowed   possessing considerable income or assets

writing naked   an option seller's strategy whereby the underlying security is not owned by the trader

WHAT KIND OF TALK IS THAT? QUIZ NO. 2
In what subject or field are the following terms used?

sextolet	f-hole
bazoo	flutter tonguing
schiettamente	con fuoco
dynamic curve	inverted mordent
fingerfertigkeit	G string

Answer on page 228.

She is teaching a class of
young boys all about contrapositives
and likes to expose their fallacies.

Dinner Toast or Prime Roast?

Saying nice things about people should be a simple matter. But evidently this isn't always so, and the praise may not even be appreciated. Such was the experience of Mr. Billings Gately.

The Gladhanders of America, a national fraternal organization, recently held a dinner to honor one of its older members, Joseph Witherspoon, and his wife, Mary. Billings Gately, an old friend of the Witherspoons, was one of the speakers. Gately's words seemed entirely laudatory. Yet his speech brought gasps from the audience, and the Witherspoons themselves were observed to have pained expressions on their faces. Only hours after Gately had left the dais—there were a few hesitant claps but mostly a tense silence—he was summarily expelled from the Gladhanders by board members. Yet curiously, after Gately's speech, there was reportedly much talk of expelling instead Joe Witherspoon!

Because the Gately speech has achieved some notoriety, we are happy to reproduce it here. You may judge for yourself the merit of what a local newspaper reporter called Gately's "full-stream paean on the Witherspoons."

■   ■   ■

Ladies and gentlemen, it's a great honor to be part of this tribute to Joe Witherspoon and his wonderful wife, Mary. Charity and public service is their real name. What can I add to what's already been said? Only that I've known Joe and Mary as long as anybody, and there are certain facts you should know about these two unregenerate altruists.

Even as a child Joe had uncurbable tendencies toward precocity. At one point he was continually adulating another boy at a school assembly, and his father was called. The whole family was impecunious, and Joe frequented areas of destitution. For a while he did backbreaking lifting work and was a laden roustabout. Only a few years after college he was living a life of open prosperity. Soon Joe was engaged in virtually indiscriminate philanthropy. Unknown to most people, there were many startling allocations. Joe didn't have the smallest peccadillo. He got a reputation for his magnanimous endowments and fiscal intercourse.

It wasn't long before a well-rounded college girl, already maturating, heard about this remarkable young man. No mystery, Mary was eminently scrutable, with a reputation as a kempt woman. Of course there were ups and downs and ins and outs in their courtship, but no breastbeating. Joe was at first wary of Mary's known perspicuity around town, but in time he grew to like her tartness. He dreamed of invigorating her. Some years earlier Mary had been highly solicitous to a community of homeless men. She was also for a while a confirmed thespian and even performed once or twice for money.

As for Joe, we all know he was prickly and refused in any way to be circumscribed. He was also rectitudinous. They didn't always see eye to eye, and Mary at times grew weary of Joe's incredulities and intimations. She even had thoughts of querying him. Others witnessed their mutual perturbation in public places. Very suggestive, Joe was easily aroused, and you never knew when he would have an eruption. But by and by, he began to respond to Mary's feverish urgings. At last, with gentle masterstrokes, he solicited her consent and introduced her to hymeneal rites. Joe quickly appreciated her cleaving.

As a couple today, Joe and Mary still live selflessly, offering hortatory advice and helping others get their fears allayed. Meanwhile, their many children and relatives, despite frequent discouragement, are carrying on all over the world.

Their oldest, Cindy, has really put herself out in Africa, where people are practicing mendicants and will do anything for food. She continues to ministrate profusely and has become an expert in famine protection and famine hygiene. The unfortunates she oversees don't eat much. Sometimes the few native cooks marinate compulsively. There is too little money and too many children, but Cindy has continued to make IOU's available for native women.

Timothy, once an apologetic pedagogue, is now a procurator, helping to manage the affairs of others.

Sandra is an architect for the military. Her shapely barracks are admired by servicemen all over the country. She is also greatly concerned about crumbling erections in cities and has recently engaged in restitution in St. Louis. Sandra has openly advocated homogeneity in the armed forces.

Arnold is a declared dramaturge, eager to touch people. He is also an impersonator, and has a number of bosom friends who are insatiable for general simulation.

Young Edward admits to being an eager interlocutor and prognosticator.

Joe's nephew Jake, a declared proselyte at a religious institution, was recently exonerated of currying secular favors. He has become interested in corrections and in having a new penal facility.

Richard, whose wife noticed that he was more and more infirm, recently went to a venerable specialist. While he was there, the doctor also took a good look at his wife's angina. Claims that Richard is a hemophiliac are untrue.

Joe's granddaughter Amelia was very young when she lost her vivacity. She got it back. Meanwhile, she has been orating and perorating but often has troubles with her rostrum.

Joe's grandson Peter secretly reads calligraphy. He and his late sister, Cornelia, had an impetuous relationship, yet he was never guilty of calumny.

In conclusion, the words of praise you have heard tonight for Joe and Mary are utterly and categorically unexceptionable. They continue to forswear sin and filth. They have also gone on record as advocating postmarital relations. Now happily retired, Joe likes golf and often plays a round. Mary, for her part, has grown interested in philosophy and logic. She is teaching a class of young boys all about contrapositives and likes to expose their fallacies.

WHAT KIND OF TALK IS THAT? QUIZ NO. 3
In what subject or field are the following terms used?

leg glance   jerker
buttery   in-swinger
cock up   rubber
goose match   spanker
hooker

Answer on page 228.

Cleavage and Intertonguing Test

In colleges and universities, certain departments or majors seem more appealing to freshmen and sophomores than others do.

A professor at Bessemer University in Pennsylvania knew just how to attract students to courses in his small department: with a taste of the exciting terminology used in his field. He accomplished this by allowing the following old "midterm test" to be "stolen" from his office. (Not being a genuine test, it would certainly not require having a proctor by the testees.) Student enrollments in his department's courses soon quadrupled.

Which courses? What subject?

See if you can guess. (Answer on page 33.)

MIDTERM EXAMINATION

1. Differentiate succinctly between bedding-plane cleavage, strain-slip cleavage, a doubly plunging fold, false cleavage, and a frost-heaved mound.

2. If you didn't want to encounter a bar finger, to what kind of place would you go?

3. Explain what "stripped plain" and "circumdenudation" describe.

4. Discuss the causes of either (a) a friction crack or (b) a gash fracture. Is either related to entry pressure?

5. If you were to do some exciting field work, which of the following phenomena would you choose to investigate and why? Explain.

    primarumpf   cycle of denudation   pimple mound
    slickenslide   penetration twin   contorted bedding

6. Distinguish between the terms *interfingering, intersertal,* and *intertonguing.*

7. Identify (a) fuggerite and (b) smectite.

8. In 25 words or less (choose one of the following), where would you be most likely to encounter (a) back thrusting, (b) Arbuckle orogeny, or (c) a clastic dike?

9. Give some possible explanations or causes for mounds having dramatic uplift.

10. Briefly, indicate why you might like to host a radio program devoted to this field.

GLOSSARY

Arbuckle orogeny a middle Paleolithic deformation

back thrusting a thrust (or strain in the crust of the earth) faulting toward the interior of a mountain-making belt

bar finger a long and narrow body of sand

bedding-plane cleavage cleavage parallel to the surface that separates layers

circumdenudation erosion that isolates an object

clastic dike a tabular formation cutting across a sedimentary formation's bedding

contorted bedding convolute lamination, or layers intricately crumpled or folded

cycle of denudation a cycle of erosion

doubly plunging fold a type of fold in the earth that reverses its direction

entry pressure displacement pressure

false cleavage fracture cleavage, occurring when fine-grained rocks split along closely spaced parallel planes

friction crack a short crack in glaciated rock transverse to the direction of ice movement

frost-heaved mound a stone ring

fuggerite a green mixture of akermanite and gehlenite

gash fracture a small-scale tension fracture

interfinger to grade or pass from one material, through interpenetrating wedge-shaped layers, into another

intersertal said of the texture of a porphyritic igneous rock of a certain type

intertonguing interlocking

penetration twin a twinned crystal

pimple mound a sandy loam dome of the Gulf Coast

primarrumpf landscape or plains that are upwarped and progressively expanding

slickenslide a polished and striated rock surface

smectite a green claylike mineral

strainslip cleavage   a rock fracturing that is a small-scale faulting
stripped plain   a plain with a flat stratum for a floor and above
   which erosion has removed weaker rocks
uplift   an uplifting of the earth's surface

■   ■   ■

Answer to "Cleavage and Intertonguing Test": Geology

■   ■   ■   ■   ■   ■   ■   ■   ■

AFRICAN FANTASY TOUR!

Visit the Dark Continent with us for six thrilling weeks totally off the beaten trek. Divagate and peregrinate shamelessly to your heart's content! You will visit:

El Kuntilla and Fuka in Egypt
El Assa in Libya
Donga and Fuka in Nigeria
Humpata, Noqui, and the Cuntuinga River in Angola
Bangem in Chad
Kaka, Bangjang, Pap, and Dongola in Sudan
Wankie District in Zimbabwe
Cess River in Liberia
Dicks Head between Somalia and Kenya
Dunga in Zanzibar
Tit Oasis and Twat (region) in Algeria
Ginchi and Titta in Ethiopia
Fougamou in Gabon
Kuntaur in Gambia
Shatshikwekwe in Zaire
Hankey, Kocksoord, and Hole in the Wall in South Africa

FOR DETAILS AND BOOKINGS, CONTACT GLOBE-TROTS TRAVEL AGENCY

■   ■   ■   ■   ■   ■   ■   ■   ■

WHAT KIND OF TALK IS THAT? QUIZ NO. 4

In what subject or field are the following terms used?

cock pose   bull posture
great penetrator   fetus pose
womb seal   gas ejector
shit process

Answer on page 228.

Calvin, age 31, has been an
itinerant chick sexer for many years.

Titular
Discrimination

As if the state of the economy weren't bad enough, many hard-working blue-collar wage-earners have encountered a disturbing new phenomenon: job-title discrimination.

Take the example of Larry X. Larry is a young man who knows how to swing a butt chain and bitch chain. He knows the ins and outs of a crotch-tongue and a swingdingle. Larry had a solid reputation as a cat hooker and ballhooter, could handle crotch grabs or a snatch team, and was a legend in hot logging when he lost his job. He properly listed these qualifications on his résumé, but was subsequently denied interviews by a record thirty-seven employment agencies. Not only that, he was barred from admission to the premises of several agencies and was visited by numerous local vice-squad investigators.

The job-title stigma suffered by Larry X is but one example among many of titular misapprehension, or semantic vocational hazards. Most victims have been members of the blue-collar community. Their job designations are all perfectly legitimate, as attested to by the listings in the U.S. Department of Labor's

Dictionary of Occupational Titles. Yet they are shunned by so-called human resources personnel.

The people named below are all plaintiffs in the historic class-action suit spearheaded by Larry X. Their job titles and livelihoods are exactly as listed in our government's *Dictionary of Occupational Titles.*

■   ■   ■

Ed M., age 37, whose plant closed two years ago, has been unable to find work as an abrasive mixer or mingler operator.

Alice T., age 24, is a recently unemployed ball sorter.

Bill M., age 51, has been flailing about trying to get rehired as a beater room supervisor.

Marge F., age 32, is into leather and has credentials as a belly roller.

Rosita P., age 29, recently arrived in the United States but is a skilled blow-off worker.

Arnold B., age 40, who has always "felt behind," would like to continue plying his trade as a bottom buffer; he has also worked as a wrinkle chaser.

Eileen K., age 33, still seeks work as a back washer.

Ben L., age 57, has considerable experience as a bunghole borer.

Alice N., age 31, has three years' experience as a fly dresser.

Vito D., age 25, has been out of work for two years as a cement shoes bottom pounder, also known as a jollier.

Betty S., age 29, is a recently unemployed cover stripper.

Jim C., age 34, was formerly a flusher but is now trained as a porcelain slusher.

Monica Z., age 24, has stiffened her resolve to find work again as a hardener helper after a brief period as a sponge hooker.

Bob G., age 33, was laid off in three different industries as an impregnator and is now interested in being a wad impregnator.

Veronica B., age 36, misses being a lace stripper but has temporary work as a lusterer.

Timothy I., age 51, is eager to again use his skills as a lag screwer.

Arnold O., age 44, has for three years been seeking further work as a leak-gang supervisor.

Beatrice L., age 50, has twelve years' experience as a nut chopper but would like to be a maturity checker.

Carol W., age 26, knows she can only go so far and would be happy to continue working as a necker.

Ted Z., age 39, a former pickup man, now seeks employment as a nibbler operator.

Madeleine B., age 27, has experience both as a rubber tester and a wink-cutter operator.

John D., age 32, used to be a layboy tender but now seeks a position as a slitter-creaser-slotter operator.

Jane C., age 30, pleased both of her former employers as a sequins slinger.

Juanita E., age 36, misses her old job as a scutcher machine taker-off.

Randolf P., age 31, still seeks work as a poke-in (or stick-in).

David P., age 46, has a lifetime's experience as a tipple worker.

Lyle B., age 30, misses his work as a wet-end helper.

Elaine E., age 28, was a latex stripper.

Kenneth L., age 39, has been in women's wear as a boner for many years.

Calvin P., age 31, has been an itinerant chick sexer for many years.

Ernest L., age 40, until recently has been a rump sawyer but hopes to go back to being a side splitter.

Seraphina Y., age 26, feels she has much to learn but has plenty to offer as a body coverer.

Melvin C., age 34, considers himself a "man of all trades"

and has experience as a gore inserter, tongue presser, and breast buffer.

Arnie H., age 35, is tired of being a drip-box tender and will accept an entry-level position anywhere.

Oliver M., age 28, likes to work with others and is qualified as a gang-vibrator operator.

Walter O., age 24, is young but eager to be a respected hooker inspector.

Sally T., age 36, is a bed operator but is thinking of moving west to become a sack-department supervisor.

Angela B., age 27, is a nut steamer.

Anna M., age 35, could use a hand up as a pump-erector helper.

Tom Z., age 30, has worked in different fields and has skills as a rod-puller and coiler and as a pull-out operator.

June N., age 27, is a rubber attacher but has also earned a livelihood as a zipper setter.

Wally H., age 31, is fascinated by time and wants to continue to make a living as a screw supervisor.

Joseph K., age 35, wants to get back to his wad-beating work as a sagger-maker's bottom-knocker.

John L., age 28, prides himself on his esprit de corps and is a stoner.

Donald F., age 34, who "wants to can rather than be canned," is a slimer.

Paul B., age 30, feels somebody somewhere has desperate need for a lingo cleaner.

GLOSSARY

abrasive mixer   a person who tends a machine that mixes abrasive compounds

back washer   the tender of a textile machine that purifies sliver

ball hooter   a logger who rolls logs down slopes

ball sorter   the operator of a machine that sorts metal balls

beater room supervisor   an overseer of pulp beating and refining before processing into paper

bed operator   a tender of equipment that transfers rolled steel shapes from processing lines to cooling beds

belly roller   an operator of a leathermaking roller machine that smooths belly hides

bitch chain   a short hook-and-ring logging chain used in loading

blow-off worker   a worker in compressed and liquefied gases

body coverer   one who fits and glues fabric covering to caskets

boner   one who inserts bone in corsets

bottom buffer   one who buffs shoes and boots

bottom pounder (or **jollier**)   in boot and shoe production, one who tends a machine that smooths edges of leather uppers

breast buffer   in boot and shoe production, one who tends a machine that smooths or roughens the forepart of the shoe's heel

bunghole borer   the operator of a machine that bores holes in casks or barrels

butt chain   a logging chain used to attach the end of a trace to a singletree (a pivoted swinging bar) in a harness

cat hooker   one who fastens choker cables around logs

chick sexer   a person who examines chick genitalia to determine sex

cover stripper   the operator of a machine that puts protective or decorative paper on boxes

crotch grabs   a V-shaped log shackle, consisting of two hooks chained to a ring

crotch-tongue   two pieces of wood forming a V between the front and rear parts of a logging sleigh

drip-box tender   in corn products, one who positions the spout of a portable tank containing starch solution over boxes lined with cloth and opens a valve to fill each box, and later removes solid starch cakes for the kiln

fly dresser   one who makes artificial flies for anglers

gang-vibrator operator   the operator of a concrete paving machine

gore inserter   in boot and shoe production, a worker who uses a stitching machine to insert a triangular or tapering piece

hardener helper   an assistant in tempering watch parts

hooker-inspector   a textile worker who uses a hooker machine that folds cloth and examines the cloth for weaving or finishing defects

hot logging   logging whereby logs go from the stump right to the stream landing or mill

impregnator   one who controls equipment that impregnates (seals or insulates) electronic components

lace stripper   a worker who tends a textile trimming and embroidery machine

lag screwer   the operator of a furniture-making machine that inserts lag bolts in table legs

latex stripper   one who strips molded latex or plastic products (such as masks, footwear, or puppets) from molds

layboy tender   an operator of a paper stacking and counting apparatus

leak-gang supervisor   a supervisor who watches for light, heat, or power leaks

lingo cleaner   a textile worker who cleans metal lingos (weights attached to cord in a type of loom apparatus)

lusterer   a worker who gives luster to textiles

maturity checker   the operator of a canning-and-preserving machine that mashes and grades peas

mingler operator   one who mixes raw sugar and syrup

necker   in jewelry-case making, one who feeds rolls of fabric and cardboard into a machine that forms cardboard necks (fillers in the jewelry-box lining)

nibbler operator   one who operates a machine that cuts metal plates into shapes

nut chopper   one who feeds a machine that chops nuts

nut steamer   a worker who immerses nuts in hot water to facilitate the shelling process

pickup operator   a textile inspector of gray corduroy

poke-in a steelworker who handles bars with tongs

porcelain slusher one who tends dipping tanks to coat articles with paint, stain, molten tin, etc.

pull-out operator a person who pulls out sheets of dried felt-base floor covering from racks in the drying oven

pump-erector helper in construction, the assistant to a worker who installs and repairs submerged turbine pumps in water wells (using truck-mounted rigs)

rod puller and coiler in production of nonferrous metal alloys, one who tends a device that coils hot rod, wire, and tubing from an extrusion press or rolling mill

rubber attacher one who glues rubber in the manufacture of sports equipment

rubber tester one who uses gauges to test rubber compounds and goods

rump sawyer in slaughtering, one who cuts hind pieces

sack-department supervisor an overseer of workers who handle cartons, sacks, and twine for grain and feed mill supplies

sagger-maker's bottom-knocker a pottery-ware worker who uses a heavy wooden tool to beat out a wad of fireclay (clay used for firebrick and crucibles)

screw supervisor one who oversees activities of workers engaged in fabricating watch screws

scutcher machine taker-off one who removes hemp fibers from a machine conveyer in making cordage and twine

sequins slinger one who tends a machine that interlaces thread around strings of sequins

side splitter in slaughtering and meat packing, one who splits sides of meat

slimer one who removes slime from fish preparatory to canning

slitter-creaser-slotter operator one who sets up and operates a machine to slot, score, crease, and trim corrugated or plain paperboard sheets

snatch team a logger's extra team of draft animals for use in difficult hauling situations

sponge hooker   a gatherer of sponges from the sea bottom by
   means of a pole with a hook

stoner   one who smooths enamel articles of jewelry

swingdingle   a type of single logging sled

tipple worker   one who tends mechanical or electronic dumping
   equipment, as from railroad cars into bins

tongue presser   the tender of a machine that shapes and removes
   wrinkles from the tongues of shoes

wad impregnator   one who tends tumbling barrels that put wax
   into shotgun-shell filler wads

wet-end helper   one tending the wet end of a machine that cuts
   and paints wallboard

wink-cutter operator   the operator of a machine that cuts rubber
   into specified lengths and weights for footwear outsoles

wrinkle chaser   one who irons wrinkles out of shoes

zipper setter   the operator of a sewing machine equipped with
   guides that prevent the needle from contacting metal in making
   slide fasteners for mattresses, blankets, cushions, etc.

WHAT KIND OF TALK IS THAT? QUIZ NO. 5
In what subject or field are the following terms
used?

bustamite	dike rocks
Knoop hardness	lingula
penetration twins	dickite
coal balls	pinacoidal cleavage

Answer on page 228.

Groined Premises

The language of architecture could be called edificial. But edifying?

What better way to get a feeling for old stonework than to rent an old British castle for a month?

At the office of a Scottish estate agent, or realtor, the following was one of several descriptive notices recently posted to attract wealthy American couples interested in a summer's touch of ye olde Britain.

McBallock Castle, the realtor tells us, is still available. Apparently most prospective renters who have read the notice below decided it might be too improper or exhausting a place to live in even temporarily.

McBALLOCK CASTLE

Fantastic old Scottish bulwark on seacoast for summer rental!

This adulterine castle—shades of Coity!—is surrounded by

virgin forest and ample old breastworks. A most homey bastion, built by a nineteenth-century English architect-engineer who throughout the British Isles had piles of note. Solid fundament, and part of it hard core. The present owner is an armor devotee and has a cuirass. He is always poking his face into a beaver and likes to get it on under a basinet.

The main part of the very eclectic structure is an impregnable peel tower, now with weather stripping and strip lighting. Atop the curtain, you'll find a real allure and close embrasures. Downstairs very stable, as cattle used to be kept there. Note the unique diapering and relieving arch. Now a mess for the staff. Pien check at the steps and a priest's hole to see just past the rear arch and the old pew.

Largely fornicate living quarters and buttery upstairs, with old cocket centering, notable groining, and tooling, and no redundant members. The central room is sexangled—nooky everywhere—with solid reveals. Attractive kiss marks on the bricks. You will see a Lesbian cyma, a cyma recta, an attractive vesica piscis, and some interesting necking as well as a rampant arch. The foliage on the tracery is sexfoils but that outside, decorating the raking lines, is a crocket.

Young woman lives on nearby hill close to remnants of a medieval cat house. Privileges do not extend to the shack up there.

The fortunate renter will also be privileged to see the heraldic devices of the owner's family displayed at various places throughout the castle. The unusual McBallock coat of arms, which are arms of affection, show a peasant erect, two wenches addorsed, and a fructed cherry. There is a couple-close, with undee ordinaries, a filly caboshed, a quail trussed, and a mermaid urinant.

The architect remains unknown, but one cannot help but admire his impressive and long-standing erection.

GLOSSARY

addorsed (heraldry) back to back

adulterine erected without a royal license

allure a wall-walk atop a curtain

arms of affection (heraldry) arms assumed out of gratitude to a benefactor

basinet a light steel helmet often having a point

beaver an armor piece for the lower part of the face

breastwork a temporary or improvised fortification

buttery a storage place for wine and ale

caboshed (heraldry) representing an animal's head "affronte" without the neck showing

cat house a medieval defensive structure that was low and movable

cocket centering a type of arch centering using special bracing rather than a horizontal tie beam

Coity a castle in Glamorgan, Scotland

couple-close (heraldry) a chevron having only one-fourth of a chevron's usual breadth

crocket in Gothic architecture, a small bump on the multi-polygonal edges of a pyramidal projecting

cuirass an armor piece covering the body from neck to waist

curtain connective fronting, or a wall, between two bastions

cyma recta an S-shaped curve molding

diapering a geometric design

embrasure a door or window recess, or a flared parapet opening for a cannon

erect (heraldry) upright

fornicate arched or vaulted in form

fructed (heraldry) bearing fruit

fundament a building foundation

groining using groin vaulting (where intersecting vaults form a curved line) or a series of such vaults

hard core broken stone, brick, etc., used for foundations or roads

kiss marks   brick discolorations sometimes used ornamentally

Lesbian cyma   a cyma reversa, or double-curve projecting molding with the convex part projecting farther than the concave part

mess   dining place; refectory

necking   a small molding atop a column or pilaster

nooky   having recesses or nooks

ordinary   a common geometric mark on an escutcheon

peel tower   a small but massive tower (with the dwelling above, cattle below)

pien check   a type of cut groove or channel made in an edge, as in steps

pile   any building

priest's hole   a secret place once used to hide priests

raking lines   lines that angle or slope away from the perpendicular

rampant arch   an arch one of whose abutments or imposts is higher than the other

redundant member   a member (in a framed structure) unnecessary for support

relieving arch   an arch above a lintel to distribute the weight of the wall above (also, discharging arch)

reveal   a wall to the side of a door or window

sexangled   hexagonal

sexfoil   in Gothic tracery, a six-lobed foliation

tooling   stone dressing

trussed   (heraldry) folded (wings)

undee   (heraldry) waved or wavy (lines)

urinant   (heraldry) diving

vesica piscis   a pointed oval form or aureole

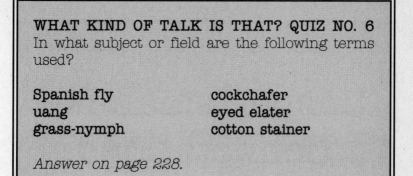

WHAT KIND OF TALK IS THAT? QUIZ NO. 6
In what subject or field are the following terms used?

Spanish fly	cockchafer
uang	eyed elater
grass-nymph	cotton stainer

Answer on page 228.

Unsportsmanlike Connotations

Scoring is the main goal in virtually all sports, and there's only one other activity in which that word is used to signal success. Does this tell us something? Maybe not. Or maybe it suggests that the language of athletics—or media athletics—and that of more private or taboo human activity might easily be interchangeable.

It wouldn't take a private eye to prove that the often provocative lingo of football, basketball, and baseball—the Big Three—might not be at all out of place in pulp fiction. In such a different context, these terms can be more than a little suggestive. As when dropped in an unsportsmanlike way into, say, a hardboiled private-eye narrative?

THE MALTESE THREE-LETTER MAN

One by one I watched the nicely rounded Turkish dance applicants leave the neoned Café Ankara, a belly series of nubile hopefuls going back out into the rain.

I was staking out the ratty Levantine bistro, known for its clipping, for my partner. I wasn't one to blow a coverage, even when the hashhouse food I had just eaten was turning into an ambitious stomachache.

It was just another down-and-dirty case for Marlin Spade. I was still putting the pieces together. So far it had the makings of a bad play, one so bad it wasn't even being reviewed.

The tall one called Sonia exited maybe an hour before the milkmen began their rounds, and alone. The Neanderthal in the beret who specialized in unnecessary roughness wasn't with her, so I fell into step. She turned right. If she was going all the way, she was headed for the Hotel Cairo, a real flea-flicker. There, unknown to Sonia Lavoris, one Ellsworth Gritch, sporting a neat red hole in his forehead, lay blown dead on her dressing table. If he had thrown up a Hail Mary, it hadn't worked. In his pockets I had found only three pieces of paper, each bearing a letter of the Greek alphabet. You figure it. Had Gritch belonged to I Phelta Thi?

Sonia Lavoris was definitely female. I watched the movement of her tight, drenched raincoat over her spread end and my pure thoughts went into naked reverse. For a navel wiggler, she was typically plumply pleasing and had a balanced line and quick slants, though I'd heard she had once been punched around so much she had worn a nose guard. Though many had doubtless been between the uprights, I'd also heard she didn't give it away and was always in the pocket. Who gets free kicks? But I always regarded myself as a pretty fair catch. And I had my tried-and-true nickel defense: "Five bucks is all I can spare at the moment . . ."

A worn-out shamus shouldn't dream, but as I followed her I broke my wishbone wide open. Was she about to make me a swing pass?

Near some embassy building—flags all over—she dropped a gum wrapper on the sidewalk next to a trash container. At least she hadn't thrown into traffic.

It had been a hard day. I began to daydream about Sonia Lavoris. I imagined that fleabag room with the body in it.

*She was staring at my fly pattern, and worried about my be-
ing just short. She was stripped and whispering to me about her
center snap and double-slot formation. I was talking to her and
sensing no immediate penetration—I'd make my point after—and
that was even more exciting. Would it just be a two-minute drill, a
bump and run? Whichever, I'd go for it. Then I thought of her
large male companion with the beret. In size he was a huddle in
one. Was she also into French tacklers? Piling on?*

Sonia Lavoris continued straight ahead toward the Hotel
Cairo. Her raincoat flapped but all I could hear was swish, swish.
I pictured her younger, in a loose pull-up jumper and tight pull-
down pants. Like any guy, I pictured her pleasantly unbright, even
dribbling a little. I visualized her eager to give an assist, to call me
for traveling, offering me her hot hand, whispering to me secrets
about ball handling and a certain gentle zone press and something
exciting called a finger roll. I saw her welcoming a two-on-one, a
triple double, but I was selfish.

Then the dreamland doubts chimed in. I couldn't stop
fantasizing.

*We were in that tiny hotel room, just a box and one fire es-
cape. Gritch's body was as cold and blue as Mineral Ice. One
liver-spotted hand still gripped a snub-nosed .38. Had he tried to
get off a desperation shot?*

*She usually asked fifty dollars a throw, word was. I was
counting on a free throw. I just wanted to be her pick and roll with
her. Suddenly she was charging, talking about penetrating her zone
and a "violation," and mentioning some thirty-second rule of hers.
She was threatening to bring it up before a real down court. I
grabbed for her baggy-stockinged leg but hit nothing but net.
Meanwhile, I had eaten bad food and I was throwing up garbage.
I knew I'd probably have to go into a stall soon. Gritch's body
was gone from the room, carried out by half a dozen dark figures.
I knew five of them, but who was the sixth man? We were drinking and suddenly she was banging the glass. She "needed a big
man." Somebody was at the keyhole, and I could hear the rustle*

of a moving pick. All of a sudden I wanted a way out, a back-door play . . .

It was almost dawn. The newspaper bundles were hitting the corners and young hoods and doxies, as if leaving a long ball, or maybe a bad hop, were out swinging. Rather than swing here, I wished they'd swing away.

I followed Sonia Lavoris into the lobby of the Hotel Cairo. My partner had told me to "guard the bag," but she was definitely no bag and I wasn't coming up just for a cup of coffee. Riffraff and lowlifes were all over the lobby. I hated the hit men, pickpockets, and spitters, and I didn't go for the fences, either.

Sonia disappeared into the elevator, but her curves were still hanging in the air. As I passed the desk, the clerk popped up, holding a New York sirloin up to a sizable shiner around his left eye. I asked him for Miss Lavoris's magic number and recommended he try instead a Baltimore chop or some barbecued ribbies.

The bandbox elevator arrived, not loaded up but with the cleaning lady's pails on it. I was just stepping into the box when the two meatheads approached me with tools of ignorance in hand. One was well dressed and grinned. They weren't here for a cup of coffee, either, much less to set the table. I could guess they didn't plan on my elevator ride being a round-tripper or on staying for a nightcap. Somehow I didn't choke up, but no question these were heels.

At me, there was immediately a unanimous swing from the heels. They both missed. The one who then tried to jump me had evidently missed spring training and spreadeagled right out the open hallway window. The one in the suit brought out a sawed-off shotgun. But it was no speed gun. While he was working on the pumping motion I found the handle of the elevator, kicked the carpet (while holding the runner), and got his foot in the bucket. My heater was already out and it was a quick bang-bang play. Guess who had the stopper. I rolled him into the hallway and ground out my cigar on his beeper.

When the elevator reached the third floor, I was ready for a change of pace, and Sonia Lavoris had opened her door. With her room so handy, why ask her if she wanted to step out?

Gritch's body was nowhere to be seen. But I was concentrating on Sonia. Some middle relief was needed and I was warming up.

She was wearing a fall classic, and it had been a sparse fall. I walked in, but there was no advance—it wasn't necessary. She got a bottle of the hard stuff out and soon we were having a slugfest. Her breasts weren't exactly in the grapefruit league, but I would have applied to be her chest protector. Maybe I'd get a tape-measure shot—you could bet she'd put up some pretty good numbers. She was also an unquestionable leg hit.

She lit a cigarette and smiled: She had caught me looking. I wanted her to blow smoke. I was hoping I wouldn't have to make some wild pitch and risk a blooper. Luckily, her perfume was saying whiff to me and her eyes were nothing but a take sign. I was ready to take her and show her my slider. I eyed the old Murphy bed, a stand-up double. She smiled a few times, toeing the rubber. Finally she asked if I liked playing in the hole.

But she was a broad, and first I had to hear her life story. My stance on this was always open.

She started down memory lane. How her mother's pies had never been sweet enough so she jammed the batter. How her hard-working old man was killed not in a casual job action but in a called strike. How their old country porch had a defective, inside-out swing. How she worried about never being married, about always being an old broken bat, single. I finally got around to using my best line. There was nothing like a line score.

We soon got down to business, and she was taking all the way. I got to first base, and she wasn't even guarding second, third, or home. She had great angles, and I liked nibbling at the corners. I found the sweet spot. She was solid up the middle, and I had a real hummer. I had just gotten into scoring position when she sobbed and confessed I wasn't the first. She started in talking about the three others but named only two. Who had been the third sacker?

Then she began whispering about something promising called a fungo circle . . .

GLOSSARY

assist   (basketball) credit for contributing to a field goal

back-door play   (basketball) a play in which one slips behind the defense to receive a pass near the basket

bad hop   (baseball) a hit due entirely to a fluke bounce of the ball

balanced line   (football) an offense aligned with the same number of players on either side of the center

ball handling   (basketball) skill in dribbling or passing the ball

Baltimore chop   (baseball) a hit ball that is "topped" so that it bounces high and often results in the batter reaching first base

bang-bang play   (baseball) a very close play

banging the glass   (basketball) actively rebounding

belly series   (football) a series of running and passing plays that all begin with a handoff or faked handoff

between the uprights   (football) between the goalposts, as in a successful field goal attempt

big man   (basketball) the all-important tall center on a team

blooper   (baseball) a weakly hit short fly ball, sometimes resulting in a "bloop" single

blow a coverage   (football) to execute a defensive assignment poorly

blow dead   (football) to signal, by blowing a whistle, that the ball is no longer in play

blow smoke   (baseball) to pitch with overpowering speed on the ball

box and one   (basketball) a defense tantamount to a four-man zone with the fifth defender playing a dangerous scorer man-to-man

broken-bat single   (baseball) a hit made even though the bat is fractured by the pitch

bump and run   (football) a play in which a pass defender bumps his opponent before running alongside him

called strike   (baseball) an umpire-ruled strike (at which the batter has not swung)

caught looking   (baseball) struck out without having swung at the third strike

center snap   (football) the putting of the ball in play on a given down

change of pace   (baseball) a slow pitch thrown with a motion intended to deceive the batter

charging   (basketball) a physical-contact foul by an offensive player

chest protector   (baseball) frontal protection worn by a catcher or home-plate umpire

choke up   (baseball) to grip the bat handle high up or away from the narrower end

clipping   (football) illegal charging, from behind and below the waist, of a player not the ballcarrier

come up for a cup of coffee   (baseball) to have a very short career as a player at the major-league level

desperation shot   (basketball) a last-minute, "low-percentage" shot (so difficult that it is unlikely to go in)

double-slot formation   (football) an offensive formation using two slot backs

downcourt   (basketball) toward or near the basket at which the described team is shooting

fair catch   (football) a signaled (by the one catching) catch of a kicked ball that means the receiver will not attempt to advance the ball and is not to be tackled by an opponent or opponents

fall classic   (baseball) the World Series

find the handle, can't   (baseball) cannot field the ball cleanly and make the putout

finger roll   (basketball) a gentle, rolling-off-the-fingers shot close to the basket

flag   (football) a referee's yellow penalty flag dropped on the field

flea-flicker   (football) a play in which a double reverse is followed by a long pass

fly pattern   (football) a straight run at full speed downfield by a pass receiver

foot in the bucket   (baseball) an open batting stance, or one in which the batter's front leg is pulled away from home plate

free kick   (football) an unhindered kick, or one made behind a restraining line, such as a placekick or punt

free throw   (basketball) an awarded, uncontested shot made by a player, usually because he has been fouled

fungo circle   (baseball) either of two circles near home plate used by players or coaches

get into scoring position   (baseball) to reach second or third base

go all the way   (football) to make it all the way to the end zone for a score

go for it   (football) to go for the needed yardage on fourth down rather than to punt

go for the fences   (baseball) to swing to hit a home run

grapefruit league   (baseball) the preseason schedule of games, most of them played in Florida

ground out   (baseball) to hit the ball along the ground to an infielder and not reach first base safely

guard the bag   (baseball) to stay, as an infielder, close to one's base when a runner is on

Hail Mary pass   (football) a long and high desperation pass aimed toward a cluster of potential receivers

hanging curve   (baseball) a pitcher's curve ball that fails to break and can easily be hit

hard stuff   (baseball) hard-thrown or fast pitches

heater   (baseball) a fast pitch (and hence a fastball)

hit   (baseball) a successful reaching of at least one base

hit nothing but net   (basketball) to score a perfectly aimed basket

hitting the corners   (baseball) pitching artfully to get strikes at the edges of the plate

hold the runner   (baseball) to keep (as a pitcher) a runner close to his base

hole   (baseball) the open space between two infielders

hot hand   (basketball) an interval during which it seems a player can't miss, or has a scoring "touch," when he shoots

huddle   (football) an on-field clustering of the players to plan the next play

hummer   (baseball) a good fastball

inside-out swing   (baseball) a type of swing in which the batter's hands are to the fore when contact is made

jam the batter   (baseball) to pitch very far inside or close to the batter's body

just short   (football) barely shy (in yardage) of a first down

keyhole   (basketball) the free-throw area or lane

leg hit   (baseball) a mere infield bouncer or grounder but a hit because of the hitter's all-out running

line score   (baseball) a team-total scoring summary for a game

loaded up   (baseball) full (the bases, with runners)

long ball   (baseball) a ball hit to or over the fence

magic number   (baseball) a calculated number, based on a team's needed wins combined with an opponent's needed losses, which determines when a division championship can be assured

middle relief   (baseball) pitching from a reliever in the middle innings of a game

moving pick   (basketball) an illegal offensive screening maneuver

naked reverse   (football) a reverse in which the ballcarrier goes in the direction opposite to that of his blockers

nibble at the corners   (baseball) to pitch artfully over the edges of the plate

nickel defense   (football) a defense using five backs

nightcap (baseball) the second game of a doubleheader

no advance (baseball) no progress by a runner to the next base

nose guard (football) a middle guard, playing opposite the offensive center

open stance (baseball) a batting stance in which the front foot is farther away from the plate than the rear foot

out swinging (baseball) getting a third strike by swinging rather than taking (not swinging)

penetrating (basketball) succeeding in dribbling in close to the basket

penetration (football) movement through the opponent's line

pick and roll (basketball) a play involving the setting of a screen, or momentary obstructing of an opposing player, and a wheeling movement toward the basket to receive a pass

piling on (football) the illegal jumping of many players on a ballcarrier already down

pocket (football) the quarterback's maneuvering area behind the line of scrimmage

point after (football) the extra point that can be made after a touchdown

pop-up (baseball) a ball hit high over the infield

pull-up jumper (basketball) a jump shot made abruptly, with the shooter stopping his dribble suddenly

pumping motion (baseball) a pitcher's arm moves preliminary to delivering the pitch

put up good numbers (baseball) to hit so as to have impressive statistical totals

quick slant (football) a quick angular rush by a ballcarrier, potential receiver, or defensive lineman

review the play (football) to scrutinize (as judges) the videotape of the last play to confirm that field officials made the correct ruling

ribbies (baseball) runs batted in

round-tripper (baseball) a home run

rubber (baseball) the toe slab on the pitcher's mound

scoring position   (baseball) second or third base for a runner, from which a hit can drive him home

set the table   (baseball) to get on base so that the next batter or batters can drive in a run or runs

sixth man   (basketball) an important substitute player

slider   (baseball) a pitch like a fastball but that breaks or curves near the plate

slugfest   (baseball) a game with much hitting and scoring

solid up the middle   (baseball) having a good catcher, middle infield, and center fielder

speed gun   (baseball) a hand-held instrument to measure the speed of a pitch

spread end   (football) an offensive player positioned outside the formation to be a pass-receiving wide receiver

spring training   (baseball) preseason training

stand-up double   (baseball) a two-base hit for which the batter can reach second base standing up or relatively easily

step out   (baseball) to back out of the batter's box temporarily

stopper   (baseball) a dependably consistent pitcher or relief pitcher

stripped   (football) "relieved" of the ball by a defending player

sweet spot   (baseball) the best part of the bat for hitting a pitch

swing away   (baseball) to swing freely or as hard as one wishes (without orders to the contrary from the manager or coaches)

swing from the heels   (baseball) to get a full and mighty swing at a pitch

swing pass   (football) a swing-type pass thrown to a back running outside the formation

swish   (basketball) to make a basket cleanly without the ball touching the backboard or rim, or the sound representing hitting "nothing but net"

take all the way   (baseball) to have no intention of swinging at a particular pitch

take sign   (baseball) the secret signal for a batter not to swing at a pitch

tape-measure shot (baseball) an impressively long home run

third-sacker (baseball) the third baseman

thirty-second rule (basketball) a rule that a shot must be attempted by the offensive team within thirty seconds

throw into traffic (football) to attempt a pass to an area with a cluster of offensive and defensive players

throw up garbage (basketball) to make easy, uncontested shots, as at the close of a one-sided game

tight end (football) an offensive lineman positioned close to the tackle position

tools of ignorance (baseball) the equipment used by a catcher

traveling (basketball) the violation by a ballhandler who takes too many steps or does not dribble the ball enough in a particular move

triple double (basketball) achieving in one game ten or more points, assists, and rebounds

two-minute drill (football) calling several plays in a single huddle because of time pressures near the end of a period or game

two-on-one (basketball) a one-man advantage on an offensive break against a single defender

unnecessary roughness (football) harsh treatment of the ballcarrier, an act that is penalized

violation (basketball) a rule infraction by the team with the ball

warm up (basketball) to get ready to come into the game to pitch

whiff (baseball) to strike out

wild pitch (baseball) a pitch (not swung at) beyond the reach of a catcher

wishbone (football) a variation on the T formation

zone defense (basketball) a strategy in which players guard not opposing individuals but areas of the court

zone press (basketball) a type of limited man-to-man defense

WHAT KIND OF TALK IS THAT? QUIZ NO. 7
In what subject or field are the following terms used?

breast drill   internal vibrator
bastard pointing   sagging moment
diaphragm pump   boning rod
straddle facing   treated pile
forepump   bleeding
dumb snatch   stud finder
hand finisher   gypsyhead
hole director

Answer on page 228.

■   ■   ■   ■   ■   ■   ■   ■   ■

CANADIAN CAPERS TOUR!

No chilly receptions in this four-week tour with lots of northern exposure. Nothing bland about these picturesque destinations you'll want to tell your friends about when you get back home! You will visit:

Arseneault in Quebec

Asselstine, Caesarea, Dongola, Jockvale, Titmarsh Lake, Sixty Nine Corners, Honey's Beach, and Butt Lake in Ontario

Beavermouth, Cockmi, Kunsoot, Nude Creek, Mamalilaculla, Nukko Lake, Pinchie, Teeta, Slosh, Pete Suckers, and the Plumper Islands in British Columbia

Big Hole, Dickie Mountain, Licford, and Blowdown in New Brunswick

Black Tickle, Dildo South, Come-by-Chance, Little Bona, and Goose Arm in Newfoundland

Frenchville and Browning in Saskatchewan

Pansy in Manitoba

Pincher, Tees, and Hairy Hill in Alberta

Lower Shag Harbour, Rear Balls Creek, and Big Bon Mature Lake in Nova Scotia

FOR DETAILS AND BOOKINGS, CONTACT GLOBE-TROTS TRAVEL AGENCY

■   ■   ■   ■   ■   ■   ■   ■   ■

Do They Talk This Way in Brigadoon?

Most of us, when we think of Scotland, think of swirling kilts, skirling pipes, and magic mist. But the language of that bonnie land has not always been wee, sleekit, or tim'rous, at least, not in the Lowlands.

Scottish, or Scots, is the variety of English that is the language of Lowland Scotland and most of Scotland's major cities. (The language of the Highlands is Scottish Gaelic, also known as Scots Gaelic.) If you check a dictionary of Scots English, such as that by Alexander Warrack, you'll find that, pungent as many of our rarer or older English words are (see "Lively Dead English" on page 134), we have nothing on the earthy, Scot-ological vocables of parts of northern Britain.

■   ■   ■

ase-hole   a hole for ashes outdoors or before a grate
balling   dancing
bang-rape   a thief's rope with a noose used to steal corn or hay

beattocks mashed potatoes

bitch-fou very drunk

blown-cod a cod split and half-dried

bofft (describing grain) damaged by birds or by a long and wet harvest

bonnar a bond or mortgage

boogers the rafters of a roof

bulfart a fat person

clitie the fall of a child

cock-a-bendy a sprightly boy

cock-a-ridy to ride (as a child) on another person's shoulders

cock-raw "sparingly" roasted or boiled

come and gang give and take

coosie a difficult, daring, or dextrous feat

crap o' the water the first water taken from a well after midnight on December 31, reputed to bring good luck in the new year

crappin the crop or stomach

cundy-hole a conduit, such as one across a hole

cunt (or cont) count, or estimation

cuntack the father-lasher, a fish

doot to doubt

dowfart dull and stupid

foogie-lick a blow struck as a challenge to a fight

gutter-teetan the rock pipit, a bird

hot-trod a hounds-and-horn pursuit in old border forays

juggs (or jougs) an iron collar used to tie the neck of a criminal to a post or a wall

kinkhost whooping cough

lapster-clap a stick with an iron hook for catching lobsters at low tide

lust appetite for food

nucky a small corner; a tassel or knob on a cap; a fish hook

Peter-Dick (or Peter-a-dick) a particular rhythmic pattern or dance step

pisweip   the lapwing, a bird
prick-haste   great haste
prickmedainty   an affectedly sweet person; a fop
prick's-worth   anything of totally negligible value
pussy-bawdrons   an affectionate name for a cat
ream-pig   a jar for holding cream
rumping-shaft   a weaver's rod used for warehouse payment in advance
shittle   a shuttle
suck   a whirlpool
suckener   a feudal tenant obligated to grind his grain at a particular mill
sucky   clover; a pet name
teat   (or tait) a tuft; a small quantity of anything
testie   the black guillemot, a bird
tit   a fit of temper; mood or humor
tithand   news or tidings

WHAT KIND OF TALK IS THAT? QUIZ NO. 8
In what subject or field are the following terms used?

penetration aid
buck and ball
cross servicing
degradation
full cock
liaison
Maggie's drawers

tampion
joint servicing
touchhole
peep sight
castrametation
undress parade

Answer on page 228.

As a tender, he's got a cockboat —
be sure you don't call it
his little dinghy!

Nauti Talk

Blow me down if the lingo of sailing isn't a tricky one to master, or mistress. From the terminology of shipbuilding to the jargon of sailboating and yachting, it's one heaving, slippery deck, easily awash with unseaworthy connotations.

It makes a landlubber a little uneasy learning about such things as stays, stirrups, sextants, Mae Wests, jackrods, and heavy spirketing—and it doesn't stop there. Nautical terminology is one big dirty wind.

A landlubber going aboard a vessel for the first time could well benefit from a few tips, particularly when she is an attractive and innocent girl going aboard the *His Honey* with its wealthy owner, the notorious roué Chet Barnfield. Lily White was such a girl. She didn't know a making water from a poop royal.

But Lily was fortunate enough to have a woman friend, Abra Zeer, who had already been out on *His Honey* with Mr. Barnfield. Abra wrote the following somewhat confused note to Lily to familiarize her with some of Mr. Barnfield's dos and don'ts aboard his many-sheets-to-the-wind pleasure craft.

69

Unfortunately, Abra did not have time to explain the meanings of the various nautical terms she mentions in the following note. We've provided a helpful glossary after her letter.

■   ■   ■

Dear Lily,

I thought you might like a few tips about what Mr. Barnfield expects of those going out in his big sailing boat with him and his crew. Once you get aboard, there'll be hands all over the place—there's nothing like being surrounded by wet seamen! Always watch your step and take precautions. Many of the spars on the boat swing both ways and are dangerous.

Regarding your skipper, there's both bad news and good news. The bad news is he's a bit of a practical joker, particularly with his personal female guests (I've talked to a few other victims, too). He cautioned me there'd be bells for fire drills now and then. He made sure he called the first when I was in the shower—I rushed out on deck in a towel. The crew—Bill, Nathan, Wilkie—got quite a kick out of this!

The good news is that you'll find a *treasure* aboard! He will hide a very nice personal gift for you somewhere on the boat that you'll have to find before putting into port again. You get a "clue." My clue, he told me, was "Clear the decks and take the stowaway!" I began racking my brains. Would I find my treasure in time?

Mr. Barnfield is a nice enough person once you learn something about his boat. Everybody is expected to help out while at sea, and I did my part with some cooking in the galley. I handled the "special" meals, or what Mr. Barnfield called "laying a course for China." He also likes a girl he can depend on, say, to splay out some sheer legs when he calls for it. A former girlfriend of his had a great craft herself, and he often reminisces about her nifty afterpeak.

Remember to always refer to the boat as "she" or "her." It's sexist, but I guess that's the tradition. He's got a temper, so don't flinch if now and then you give him a little pique. One girl who came aboard really annoyed him, and he brought her right off!

And keep these points in mind.

Mr. Barnfield likes *His Honey* to put out promptly, so hit the deck fast. At the cathead, his anchor will be acockbill (he'll point out the pee, too). In port he often eats and drinks too much, and he hates the trots of crowded harbors. He's always in command and loves to adjust to any deviation. He can always hear the far ting of a buoy or, hearing an "Ahoy!," quickly discern the littlest man in a boat. Of course, it's all a matter of time, of getting a feel, of feeling your legs.

From your bow to your stern, Mr. Barnfield will try to familiarize you. When I was aboard, he was proud of *His Honey*'s sleek buttocks, and he was impatient to take me below. There he offered me quarters. Up at the bow, he was a great appreciater of curves and planking and futtocks. He told me all about his main pieces and what he considers well built.

All the while, of course, I was trying to figure out where my "buried treasure" gift was hidden. "Clear the decks and take the stowaway"? Every day I looked all over the deck of the boat. Nothing. Was there really some person aboard who was a stowaway?

Watch your step around the gutter bar! If it's windy and he offers to take you to his half-poop—that's a poop too small for a man to stand under—say no! At the fore and aft lines he may try to interest you in, say, the art of diagonal planking. He's a bit of a wag—don't let him get you all wet down below! He's so restless. One minute he'll be talking to you on the quarterdeck, and before you know it he'll be going down to the waist. If he offers to "show you the midriff," say no!

The sails, of course, are the hard part. So much sheet!

Mr. Barnfield can handle anything from breast backstays to French lugs, will prick a sail when he knows it's necessary, and is knowledgeable about breasthooks and cheek blocks. He also knows how to farthell. As for scuba, he's a little clumsy and seems to have muffed diving. So he snorkels. Don't ever sit on his face mask!

Your skipper has all kinds of small boats on board. He once asked me to be his oar! As a tender, he's got a cockboat—be sure you don't call it his little dinghy!—and, for special needs, a smelly old johnboat with paddles. He joked with me about wanting to be a cunner conner—sail a Chesapeake log canoe!—and getting his very own head. He and a friend once took me ashore in a big rowing boat in which I had my choice of sitting on either of two dickies.

You'll get to swim now and then, of course. Or be assigned on bright, sunny days to "shark watch." Some afternoons I was asked to stand in my swimsuit, with a speargun, in this little basketlike platform near the rail and keep looking through this mounted telescope at the water. I had to bend over to look through it. It turned out that they all just wanted to enjoy some good views of me in my bathing suit!

But Mr. Barnfield really showed me the ropes. (He's tied the knot more times than you can believe!) And watch out for the guys! There's always a hitch, like a lowering hitch. He's got a special thing called a pricker. For example, to keep your earing from slipping off, he'll show you his bullwhanger, and maybe tell you all about snotters, not to mention straining screws. He's had everything on board, twice-laid, hard-laid, or not, but he'll try to keep you away from the spankers and jumper guys. There's even such a thing as unlaying!

Strand for strand, Mr. Barnfield pays attention to the little things, from the firmness of the cuntline to cunt splices to throat seizings. He's read up on "the big ones," and is always watching for impressive gams—he's fearless and will head right between them! He collects sperm oil, you know, and loves to hold forth on what makes the best harpoon tang. He knows his smiting lines and is quite an expert in American whipping. Note: You're fairly small, so when it comes to bringing *His Honey* right up to some filthy wharf, let him get his hands on the breast fast.

From time to time, Mr. Barnfield is keen on bottom testing, for which he has something called a feeler. Oddly, he's always a little nervous when it comes to touching bottoms.

There are other little things, too. Between the sheave and the shell of a block, for instance, you've got your arse. Mr. Barnfield will teach you a lot about cheeks and chafing cheeks and the usefulness of a rubbing paunch, and he can fix things, whether with a crack arrester (over a stressed area) or a tingle. He's put all kinds of useful things in his lady's hole, including "roller-reefing gear"!

But where was my hidden treasure? By "clear the decks," did it mean I'd only find my gift when nobody was on deck? I gave up on that and began looking around the lifeboat, where a "stowaway" might conceivably be. My time was running out! And Mr. Barnfield always wanted my company.

He's very proud of the wood on the boat and especially partial to poon. And if you ask him what kind of fiber most of the ropes (cordage) are made from he's got a ready answer: "Imadong!" He's even knowledgeable about fucoid things like fairies'-butter.

Remember, Mr. Barnfield owns many other boats and ships of all kinds, on one of which, he says, he's got "a sizable monkey poop." "I used to work on commercial vessels," he told me. "I know all about stiffening orders and swinging berths and negotiating between two wharves or lying in a slip. I know a truly stacked tramp from a mere oiler, and I've known single-screws and twin-screws, bonjean curves and fast feluccas." (At some other port he's apparently got both a dead-rise model and a fast runabout!)

Salty history—he apparently knows his stuff there, too, from an old fish-stinking buss to a real schokker. He has all these old books aboard. He never stops talking about his dingle and a Galway hooker he once had—he much prefers well-built hookers to jackass barks—and is familiar with the fast old galleass, Nile nuggars, frigatoons, or paying for a seacunny or moorpunky in India. He's got boring drawings of an old Viking beitass and of a fuksheet. He'll tell you tales of lay days, the English customshouse circles of jerquers, suckholes, eating dandy funk, seeing a good ketch stripped to the girtline, and the old tradition of blowing the grampus. Chet's actually seen Dongola events in England, with men and women pairing up! (When he's in a racing mood himself, believe me, he knows just how much time to spend on each leg.) For the future, he's considering bareboating.

You may or may not find you like lying to. If he asks if you're into cruising or gunkholing, say yes! All in all, when it comes to the fun of boating, being out at sea is okay. But I'd much rather be tied up!

And my hidden treasure—did I find it? Yes, but only with a little more help. Mr. Barnfield told me to think of two words, "bridge" and "cabin." Then it hit me one day as I tidied up my cabin. On a high shelf were stacked sets of playing cards next to an old copy of *Uncle Tom's Cabin.* "Clear the decks and take the stowaway"? Clear the card decks and take the Stowe away! "Bridge"—card decks. "Cabin"—*Uncle Tom's Cabin!* Behind the cards and the book I found a beautiful gift-wrapped box. My treasure was a very nice diamond bracelet. Good luck with your clue!

So, courage, my dear! Don't sink, or let Mr. Barnfield go hard and fast. Never leave him hard ashore! He sometimes drinks too much, but if you're real up front, he won't go to the bottom. When he's on *His Honey* at night, it can be quite romantic. I always loved listening to a big buoy tinkling!

Slowly but surely, you'll learn all this sailing lingo. Don't be afraid of pulling a boner! But don't make the mistake I did and ask one of the guys, "What is coming about?"!

As for me, I'm now into flying and aeronautics! Ask me anything about drooped ailerons, ram pressure, forward slip, phugoid oscillation, or a snatch pickup, and I'm your girl!

Hoist the blue peter and listen for the diaphragm horn!

Abra

GLOSSARY

acockbill describing an anchor hanging free or ready to be dropped

afterpeak a ship's extreme aft compartment

American whipping a knot method for making sure that the ends of a rope do not fray out

arse the space between a sheave (pulley) and shell (case) of a block, at the other end from which the rope runs

bareboating sailing in a hired boat without a hired crew

beitass a wooden spar used on old Viking ships

blowing the grampus the tradition of throwing a bucket of cold water on a sailor who has been asleep while on watch

blue peter a blue flag used to signal that a merchant ship is ready to sail

bonjean curve certain ship's curves (or transverse section areas) used in making calculations

breast backstay on a square-rigged ship, a line from the mast's top to the deck's edges on either side

breast fast a large rope for fastening the middle of a ship to a wharf

breast hook a V-shaped steel plate or timber knee used to connect ship timbers

bullwhanger a short length of rope (nailed to the end of a yard) to prevent the earing (another rope) from slipping off

buss a rugged square-sailed boat once used in herring fishery

buttocks the aftmost, convex part of a ship

cathead a boat's bow projection, to which the anchor is raised

chafing cheeks pulleys (sheaves) at the ends of yards carrying ropes

cheek block a sheave fixed to one side of a spar

cheeks any two pieces of wood against the sides of something

cockboat a small boat used as a tender

come about to tack

conner one who steers or directs a vessel

crack arrester   a plate riveted over a crack in another plate

cunner   a log sailing canoe once common in Chesapeake Bay

cuntline   a groove formed between strands of a rope (also called cunting, contline, cantline)

cunt splice   a loop formed by a splice

dandy funk   an old sailor's food of hardtack soaked in water and baked grease with molasses

dead-rise model   a type of small high-speed power yacht

deviation   a ship-caused compass error

diagonal planking   planking where a layer of a hull's skin is diagonally fixed to the fore and aft line

diaphragm horn   foghorn

dickies   two seats at the back of a ship's larger rowing boat

dinghy   a small boat carried on a larger boat

dingle   a coracle, or primitive fishing boat of hide or oilcloth

dirty wind   confused or no wind blowing on one side of a sail

Dongola race   an English pair-as-crew boat race, often with men and women

drooped ailerons   hinged, trailing-edge ailerons on an airplane

earing   a line used for the upper corners of a sail

fairies'-butter   a blue-green alga that forms pellets or sheets

farthell   the securing of furled square sails to yards with short "farthelling" lines

feeler   a device indicating that the sounding device lead has reached bottom

feel one's legs   to gain self-confidence

felucca   a narrow and fast lateen (a ship with a certain type of rigging)

forward slip   a slight slip sideways sometimes made on an approach to landing

French lug   a balance lugsail (a four-sided sail)

frigatoon   a Venetian square-sterned sloop of war

fucoid   pertaining to algae or seaweed

fuksheet   an ancient type of sail

futtocks   pieces of a wooden ship's frame

galleass an old large and swift galley of southern Europe

Galway hooker a small Irish coastline boat

gam a school of whales

girtline a gantline, or line through a block used to hoist rigging or hang clothes

gunkholing navigating through tricky shallow channels

gutter bar the inside part of the waterway running around part of a deck

guy any guiding or bracing rope, wire, cable, etc.

half-poop a poop too small to stand beneath

hard and fast immovably aground

hard ashore fixed fast on the rocks or a beach

hard-laid (of rope) twisted tightly to a strand angle of about 45°

head a ship's toilet

hitch a temporary nooselike knot

Imadong Philippine bast fiber used in cordage

jackass bark a type of three-masted ship; also, a type of a four-masted ship

jackrod a jackstay, or a rod, bar, or rope to which sails are fastened

jerquer a customshouse officer who searched vessels for illicit or smuggled goods

johnboat a narrow, flat-bottomed riverboat usually propelled by a pole

jumper guy a line supporting the end of a bowsprit whisker (outrigger)

ketch a yawl-like vessel rigged fore and aft

lady's hole a small compartment for keeping small supplies (on big wooden sailing ships)

lay day a day allowed for loading or unloading a vessel, or a day of delay in port

leg a distinct or marked part of a course

lowering hitch a hitch used to lower one's plank "chair" while working on a mast or stay

lying to   remaining virtually motionless with the head to windward

Mae West   an inflatable yellow life jacket

main piece   a principal timber in any of several parts of a ship

making water   a boat's leaking

monkey poop   a lower and smaller poop deck

moorpunky   a large, paddle-propelled pleasure craft once used in India as a state barge

nuggar   a Nile cargo boat

oiler   an oil-cargo ship

pee   the bill (point) of an anchor

phugoid oscillation   in an airplane, long-period oscillation in the plane's longitudinal motion

poon   a hard light wood (of the poon tree) used for masts and spars

poop royal   in old ships, the highest and rearmost deck over the poop

prick   to sew an added seam between two old seams in a sail

pricker   a thin marlin spike used to make holes in sails or to open a small-diameter rope being spliced

put out   to set sail from shore

ram pressure   in airplanes, a difference between an airplane's scoop pressure (in the inlet air system) and the atmospheric pressure

roller-reefing gear   boom appliances and fittings used in a rolling (around a spar) method of reducing the area of sail presented to the wind

rubbing paunch   a piece of wood fixed to a mast (on square-rigged sailing ships) to protect yards from wear and tear

runabout   a light motorboat or speedboat

schokker   a large Dutch pleasure boat

seacunny   a steersman of India

sextant   a navigational instrument which measures altitudes of celestial bodies

sheer legs two lashed-together poles splayed out at the bottom and used for rigging a tackle to lift heavy objects

sheet sail

single-screw having one screw propeller

slip a ramped landing place for a ship

smiting line a line threaded inside ropeyarn for tying a sail to a spar

snatch pickup an airplane's hooking onto a glider, person, or object

snotter a rope on an upper yardarm

spanker a fore-and-aft sail on the aftermast of a square-rigged ship

spar any rigging boom, mast, gaff, etc.

sperm oil oil from the sperm whale

spirketing a type of planking above a wooden ship's waterways

stacked having smokestacks

stay a strong wire rope for a mast

stiffening order customs permission to receive cargo or ballast on board before permission for general loading

stirrup a type of rope secured to a yard

straining screw a type of rigging screw with a swivel hook at one end and threading at the other

suckhole a whirlpool

swinging berth a dredged basin in which vessels can be turned

tang a projecting prong or tongue connecting with a tool's handle

tender a small ferrying or communicational (with shore) boat or steamer

throat seizing a tight-wound small line used to hold two parts of a rope together

tied up moored

tingle a temporary patch over a leak

tramp a tramp steamer, or a ship not making regular trips between the same ports

trot   a way of mooring several vessels together in a harbor to save space

twice-laid   describing a rope made from parts of an old rope dis-assembled

twin-screw   having two screw propellers

unlaying   unwinding rope strands to work a splice

waist   the area between the forecastle and the poop

WHAT KIND OF TALK IS THAT? QUIZ NO. 9
In what subject or field are the following terms
used?

idle-mixture screw   ball stud
F-head   drag link
big end   choke diaphragm
fluid coupling   bar feeler gauge
petcock   sliding fit
spurt-hole

Answer on page 228.

Anton Fokker
Hazing

Remarkable names of real historical figures are also an important part of embarrassing English. Perhaps no place more lends itself to their being bandied about and kept alive than a college campus.

Fraternity and sorority initiation rites at colleges have undergone changes in recent years. Forced drinking and other dangerous stunts for pledges are out. But undergraduate Greek organizations will probably always feel that it wouldn't be fun if membership didn't hinge on some required act of personal embarrassment or self-humiliation. You can't make it *too* easy to get in. What's a fraternity to do?

It can rely on Anton Fokker hazing.

Anton Fokker hazing is a kinder, gentler hazing. It involves no direct insults to anybody. Instead, the initiate must merely introduce into conversation, in the company of frat member witnesses, any of various embarrassing names of actual historical and cultural personages. That is, these names must be of people distinguished enough—if nonetheless obscure—to be listed in a respected bio-

83

graphical reference; they are figures on whom a student could conceivably do some research.

One example of such a person is Anton Fokker, who was a Dutch airplane designer. Another is the famous Fuggers, a family of powerful German Renaissance bankers and merchants. The pledge must choose (or be assigned) such a name and confront another person with a request for some information, or how to get information, about the embarrassingly named figure.

There are five important rules in Anton Fokker hazing:

1. The pledge must use the name in a question to either (a) the most conservative member of the college's library staff, or (b) a student of the opposite sex with whom the pledge is not acquainted.
2. The pledge must articulate the name in a loud and clear voice. If he is asked to repeat it, he must again articulate it in a loud and clear voice.
3. The pledge must not spell the name in question. If asked to spell it, he or she must claim not to know the spelling and repeat the name in a loud and clear voice.
4. This conversation must be witnessed by at least two fraternity or sorority members.
5. Under no circumstances is the pledge to laugh or even smile in the course of this conversation.

For example, the hazee could presumably be doing research on English composers and ask severe old Ms. Deemly in the music library, "Have you any books on either John Blow, William Crotch, or Edmund Rubbra?"

We provide here, as a starting point, a list of historical personages (many of them from the obscure 1966 *Dictionary of Biographical Reference*) whose names lend themselves to Anton Fokker hazing.

Anullianus consul of Rome
Asser Jewish savant
John Badcock English martyr
Samuel Badcock English ecclesiastic and critic
Jens Balling Danish typographer and translator
J. S. Balls English comedian
Hermann Bang Danish novelist
Praise-God Barebone English member of Cromwell's first parliament
Bastard Majorcan painter
Sheikh Bedreddin Ottoman Empire leader of a social-religious uprising
John Blow English composer
John Henry Boner American poet and editor
James Breasted American Egyptologist
Agostino Busti Italian sculptor
Francesco Busti Roman painter
Isaac Butt Irish barrister, politician, and author
Mateo Butterfuoco Corsican general and representative
Gerard Cacapisti Italian jurist and writer
A. Cherry English actor, songwriter, and dramatist
Clitus officer under Alexander the Great
Thomas Crapper English inventor of the water closet
William Crotch English composer
Paul de Kock French novelist
Thomas Dick English writer on natural philosophy
Dongard king of Scotland
George Doo English engraver
Dudu pen name of American novelist Julia Fletcher
Eugene Fallex French litterateur
Geronimo Frigimelica Italian physicist
Peter Grosscup American judge
Arthur Harden English chemist
Richard Hole English author
Judicious Hooker English divine

Karen Horney   German-born American psychiatrist
Carl Kummer   German naturalist and geographer
Carl Kunth   German botanist
Johann Kunze   German Protestant divine and author
Benjamin Lay   English philanthropist
Louis Leakey   British paleontologist
Lech   duke of Bohemia
John Lech   archbishop of Dublin
Pietro Orefice   Italian painter
Phaloecus   Greek lyric poet and epigrammatist
Ludovic Piles   French officer and duelist
Daniel Prat   English divine and author
John Pucker   English author
Servillius Pudens   Roman consul
Edmund Rubbra   English composer and music critic
Samuel Schmucker   American Lutheran theologian
Sexred   Saxon king of Essex
William Smellie   Scottish naturalist
Sodoma   Italian Renaissance painter
Edward Stiff   American colonel and author
Arne Sucksdorff   Swedish filmmaker
Ernest Titterton   English atomic physicist
Friedrich Tittman   German historian
Jigme Wangchuk   king of Bhutan
Wang Mang   Chinese usurper

WHAT KIND OF TALK IS THAT? QUIZ NO. 10
In what subject or field are the following terms used?

pallet cock

pull-out piece screw

depthing tool

verge

impulse pin

date wheel

stud

positional timing

banking screw

vibrating tool

cracked hole jewel

meantime screw

universal head

Answer on page 228.

How Many Miles to Intercourse?

The United States has many small towns or municipalities, along with rivers, streams, and peaks, that don't make it onto most maps—purely for reasons of space. At least, they say that space is—purely—the reason for excluding many of them.

We, as a spatial interest group, take it upon ourselves to list here many of these cartographically neglected whistle-stops, state by state, and hope thereby to swell local breasts with pride. The only states not to make this list are Delaware and Rhode Island, to whose residents we offer our congratulations; or, if they prefer, our apologies.

■ ■ ■

ALABAMA: Lovelace Crossroads, Letcher, Seman, Smut Eye, Mount Willing, Pansey, Nymph, Fannie, Graball, Gay Meadows, Pulltight, Hardaway, and Trussville
ALASKA: Goose Point, Tongue Point, Point Lay, and Port Dick
ARIZONA: Cherry, Congress, Twin Buttes, and Wikieup

ARKANSAS: Peterpender, Hooker, Blue Ball, Bunn, Peel, and Delight

CALIFORNIA: Fort Dick, Hooker, Lick, Cherry Gap, Cherry Thicker, Cove, Shafter, Twin Peaks, Hole Ranch, Box Springs, Quail, Black Butte, Double Head Mountain, and Cherryland

COLORADO: Romeo, Climax Lake, Lay, Loveland, Climax, Two Buttes, and Hygiene

CONNECTICUT: Dyke Pond, Honeypot Glen, Laysville, Titicus, and Mianus

FLORIDA: Dorcas, Hardaway, Hookers Prairie, Doctors Inlet, Bare Beach, Venus, Romeo, and Hooker Point

GEORGIA: Fairyland, Split Silk, Hooker, Gay, Coosa, Boneville, Cherrylog, Between, Box Springs, Climax, Lovejoy, Clito, Butts County, Coosa, Needmore, Horns, and Inman

HAWAII: Napoopoo, Tantalus, Puu Waawaa, and Fort Shafter

IDAHO: Feely Spur, Cleft, Bone, Felt, Gay, Dingle, Standrod, and Lower Goose Creek Reservoir

ILLINOIS: Prickett, Done Gap, Dongola, Layfield, Sexson Corner, Pinkstaff, Shafte, and Honey Bend

INDIANA: Honey Creek, Strip Lake, Ballstown, Bushrod, Needmore, Gnaw Bone, and French Lick

IOWA: Dike, Balltown, Cumming, Swisher, Forbush, and Fertile

KANSAS: Reamsville, Climax, Inman, Cherryvale, Cockers Branch, Bushton, and Cummings

KENTUCKY: Big Bone, Grassy Lick, Dingus, Balls Landing, Sugartit, Plank, Bummer, Blowing Spring, Quail, Do Stop, Wicks Well, Limp, Lesbas, Letcher, Broad Bottom, Dongola, Climax, Gays Creek, Licking River, Lick Creek, Balltown, The Knobs, Knob Lick, Long Lick, Blue John, and Beaver Lick

LOUISIANA: Dykesville, Eros, Dry Prong, Cocke, Vixen, and Ball

MAINE: Bangor, Dickvale, Bunganuc Landing, Cherryfield, and Dickey

MARYLAND: Bedsworth, Onancock, Layhill, Jugtown, Blueball, Loveville, and Assawoman Bay

MASSACHUSETTS: Gay Head and Cummaquid

MICHIGAN: Climax, Leer, Cherry Hill, Peters, Gay, Romeo, and the Tittabawassee River

MINNESOTA: Flaming, Fertile, Cherry, Climax, Wangs, Kiester, Ball Club, and Two Inlets

MISSISSIPPI: De Lay, Cockrum, Love, Leakesville, Coosa, Peelers, Hooker Hollow, Service, Balls Branch, Jumpertown, Hardaway Pond, Yazoo City, Red Lick, Darling, Peekaboo, and Bangs Bayou

MISSOURI: Cherry Box, Clapper, Licking, Cockrell, Honey Creek, Anutt, Butts, Hooker, Climax Springs, Knob Lick, Shafter, Neck City, Crabbs, Dykes, Jerk Tail, Brushyknob, Couch, and Fee Fee

MONTANA: Maiden Rock, Box, Toole, Feely, and Big Hole National Battlefield

NEBRASKA: Funk and Inman

NEVADA: Shafter, Cherry Creek, Bango, Bliss, Lovelock, and Virgin

NEW HAMPSHIRE: Coos County, Center Sandwich, and Jady Hill

NEW JERSEY: Pumptown, Pullentown, Loveladies, Cream Ridge, and Cherry Hill

NEW MEXICO: Organ, Bluit, Lesbia, House, Loving, and Mount Dora

NEW YORK: Quail, Sodom, Balltown, Butternuts, Busti, Flushing, Nippletop (peak), and Vestal

NORTH CAROLINA: Cheeks, Hookerton, Fuquay-Varina, Pee Dee, Big Lick, Sodom, Boogertown, Picks, Breeches Swamp, Erect, Finger, Cane Bottom, Cumnock, Quail Roost, Bunn, Love Valley, Cherry Point, Cat Square, Blowing Rock, Nutbush (stream), Quail Ridge, and Quail Corners

NORTH DAKOTA: Dickey and Velva

OHIO: Dicks Creek, Climax, Bangs, Round Bottom, Hooker, Dorcas, Moons, Knockemstiff, Blacklick, Layhigh, Blue Ball, Mutual, Loveland, Congress, and Hooring

OKLAHOMA: Hooker, Mutual, Peek, Tushka, Box, Mons, Redden, Loveland, Felt, Mounds, and Bowlegs

OREGON: Tongue Point, Coos Bay, Peel, Hardman, Black Butte, and Dike

PENNSYLVANIA: Intercourse, Blue Ball, Climax, Muff, Keisterville, Black Lick, Lickingville, Balls Mills, Jugtown, Bareville, Venus, Gayly, Moon, and Needmore

SOUTH CAROLINA: Chick Springs, Nine Times, Hyman, Dongola, Ball Island, Venus, Peedee, Ninety Six, Cummings, and Inman

SOUTH DAKOTA: Oral, Thunder Butte, Letcher, Hooker, Bonesteel, Gayville, Nipple Butte, Slim Buttes, and Cherry Creek

TENNESSEE: Love Station, Keister, French Broad (stream), Jaybird, Bangham, Ball Play, Big Bottom, Three Way, Bone Cave, Dickey Bottom, Finger, Cherry, Nutbush, Yum Yum, Dick Cove, Graball, Vestal, Finger, Cocke County, Mount Juliet, Soddy-Daisy, Big Boy Junction, and Dickey Bluff Peninsula

TEXAS: Shafter, Titley, Needmore, Fourway, Quail, Dickworsham, Cherry Spring, Dike, Tool, Venus, Lovelady, Fuqua, Climax, Old Dime Box, Pees Ranch, Figridge, Cheek, Dripping Springs, Curvitas, Darling, Fairy, Ding Dong, Headsville, Glasscock County, Cuney, Bangs, Peters, Loving, Peeler, Peeltown, and Twin Buttes Reservoir

UTAH: Virgin, Pickelville, Strongknob, Mutual, Standrod, Black Butte, and Red Buttes

VERMONT: Hooker Hill, Honey Hollow, and Gaysville

VIRGINIA: Balls Hills, Round Bottom, Short Pump, Butts, Blowing Rock, Dugspur, Dongola, Climax, Balls Hill, Onancock, and Moon

WASHINGTON: Titlow, Nooksack, Sappho, Fairy Falls, and Humptulips River

WEST VIRGINIA: Lake Oral, Cut Lips, Lick Fork, Buff Lick, Organ Cave, Big Stick, Droop, Widemouth, Gay, Ball Gap, Dorcas, Lick Branch, and Lick

WISCONSIN: Spread Eagle, Hustler, Honey Creek, Plugtown,

Cream, Horns Corners, Gays Mills, Dickeyville, and Maiden Rock
WYOMING: Big Horn, Black Buttes, and Red Buttes

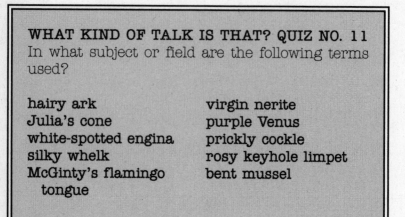

WHAT KIND OF TALK IS THAT? QUIZ NO. 11
In what subject or field are the following terms used?

hairy ark	virgin nerite
Julia's cone	purple Venus
white-spotted engina	prickly cockle
silky whelk	rosy keyhole limpet
McGinty's flamingo tongue	bent mussel

Answer on page 228.

Oz Tech
Bulletin Board

Short of having a hot date, where does an undergraduate or graduate student at Ozgood Institute of Technology go if he or she wants action?

To the giant bulletin board at the Student Union. Science students seem to have their own special terminology in posted messages. The following announcements, offers, pleas, and more were recently spotted there. Here, in the students' own inimitable words, are some prime pieces of Oz.

■　■　■

Freshpersons!
Undecided about your first-year curriculum? Take physics. It's merely a process of elimination!

Fokker-Planck study group meeting Wednesday (not Thursday), will discuss deviates, homoscedastic operations, and curved arrays.

Needed: Advice on how to make ethyl lactate. Bob, 555-0333.

Physics 101 students please do this week's paper not on the two-body problem but on the excited state.

Wanted (to teach a few eager students from Miss Parker's School): an old matrass, if anyone can spare it, and a good Kipp generator. Mike, 555-1299.

DEMONSTRATION FRIDAY AT MAJORA LAB OF LOOSE COUPLING, DIRECT COUPLING, AND SELF-EXCITATION.

The Women's Astronomy Club meeting next week will focus on the menstrual epact and vulgar establishment—not on Coma Berenices and Pump. We will also touch on the long-period variable.

Lecture Tuesday, April 20, by visiting physics professor James Rantallion, 8 p.m., Swive Hall:
   "From Magnetic Pumping to Kink Instability"

Several Kundt tubes and a very accurate balling scale are missing from the Brans-Dicke Laboratory. Please return them!

Professor Koproleit wants all Astro 21 students to know that permissible topics for this semester's term paper are (1) expertise with a Dicke-switched receiver, (2) the Trojan Group, or (3) interstellar reddening.

Lost! My double-major semester paper (researched in L.A.) on degenerate stars and irrational numbers. Reward if returned. Alex, 555-5445.

NEED TUTORING IN EXPLICIT RELATIONS? CALL 555-3448.

Can you draw? I need an illustrator for my thesis, "An Investigation of the Directrix and Poles for the Latus Rectum." Donna, 555-4118.

Ever tried mutual matriculation? Oz Tech now has inter-course credits for certain classes at Wackford University. Contact Dean's Office.

Partner needed for full-credit project involving streptasters, horny sponges, cleavage cavities, and flagellated chambers. Daryl, 555-7223.

Lecture Wednesday, April 21st, at the Glans Building, by the chairman of the biology department:
    "Vagile Organisms and the Edaphic Climax"

Used microscope for sale, perfect for graphic views of hypermastigotes, mesofurcas, suctorians, Haller's organ, etc. Carol, 555-0114.

Visiting professor Kathleen-Phyll de Joie, known for her papers on vaginicolous behavior and clitellar thickness, will give a special demonstration, after fertilization, of bilateral cleavage.

BEGINNING ZOO. STUDENTS—FOR SALE CHEAP, GREAT SLIDES OF PELVIC GIRDLES! SALLY, 555-5533.

A rare monograph on the Hooker telescope and the Lick has been stolen from the library. Not too cool.

The topic of Thursday's Witch of Agnesi Club meeting will be sextactic variations.

Anybody interested in private tutoring on ideal blackbodies and the power of Hefner candles, please call Arthur, 555-4005.

ACCOUNTING OFFICE LOOKING FOR TWO PART-TIME SECRETARIES; GOOD FIGURES. CONTACT MR. LEO NISUM, 555-2112.

For extra credit, General Science students may write on either the homosphere and homopause or on Gay Lussac's law.

Dr. Muller's special project students will present their topics at the 3:00 seminar Wednesday: Jim Carter's frontal organs, Diane Pell's anal feelers, and Josh Orstein's sex-intergrades.

Freshman or sophomore future Physics majors! I have the following used books for sale at half price (Kathy, 611-8776):

HORIZONTAL INTENSITY, THE PINCH EFFECT, AND
   THE POYNTING THEOREM
BAUDS AND THE OLD SEXTUPLEX
BRAGG'S CURVE AND THE FRENKEL DEFECT
DISSIPATION TRAILS AND INDUCED DRAG
THE HARTREE-FOCK APPROXIMATION
LECHER WIRES

AN "ELECTRIC" DEMONSTRATION OF PROFESSOR MENTULATE'S CARBON PILES WILL BE HELD THIS COMING MONDAY AT 12 NOON.

Professor Bathycolpian's class! Watch this bulletin board. Due to last week's get-together on capacity coupling being too large, we may be trying a little sectional experimentation.

The winner of this year's Algy Lagnia Prize is Jeannette Tarsy for her paper on preclimaxes and climaxes.

Notice: Both A Section and B Section of Professor Gerard's expected "Birth of the Universe" class are too large. This will necessitate a C Section.

Anybody who can fill me in on the amphipathic activity demonstrated last Tuesday, *please* call me at 555-0012. I am eager to make it up!

GRAPHIC COLOR PHOTOS OF THE VENA CONTRACTA, CORONAL HOLES, AND HEMICOLLOIDS! SEE EXHIBIT IN BASEMENT OF KARNOVSKY SCIENCE BUILDING.

Needed! Female partner for extra-credit project on the double slit experiment. Call Steve, 555-6661.

Zoo. Students—
Presentable lutrine paper for Mrs. Elliot must be turned in next *week, not this week.*

Anonymous comment: Was the visiting lecture last night on primordial outgassing a stinker, or what?

Correction:
The Oz Tech News *would like to apologize to Prof. Korstein for misreporting a statement in his Parents' Day lecture. It was not Lucy's bones that Donald Johanson jumped on at Dik-dik Hill.*

ANYBODY INTERESTED IN VERY EXPERT TUTORING IN THE ASSES BRIDGE AND SOME MEAN DEVIATIONS, PLEASE CALL DONNA, 555-2238.

Astro 22 students be advised you all have much to learn about the Big Bang. Better scores will be expected next week.

Inconsiderate Geology dweeb, whoever you are:
My lab alcove table (4A) in Whitfield is not a burial ground for your field specimens. Please get your rocks off!

GLOSSARY

anal feeler   a posterior sensory appendage in worms and insects

asses' bridge   a famous geometrical proposition: the angles at the base of an isosceles triangle are equal

balling scale   a type of hydrometer scale

baud   a telegraphy signaling unit

big bang   the theory that the universe began with a single explosion

bilateral cleavage   in vertebrates, a mitotic division that results in a bilaterally symmetrical arrangement of blastomeres

blackbody   an ideal surface or body for absorbing radiant energy

Bragg's curve   in physics, a graph for an average number of ions per unit distance along a particular beam

capacity coupling   coupling in which two circuits have a common capacitor

carbon pile   a voltaic or galvanic pile, an arrangement for generating an electric current

cleavage cavity   the cavity on an arthropod's lower body surface

climax   the fairly stable stage or community reached by an available population of organisms

clitellar   pertaining to the thickened band around segments of such annelids as the earthworm

Coma Berenices   a constellation north of the ecliptic

coronal hole   the dark and low-density part of the sun's corona

C-section   cesarean section

curved array   a number of mathematical elements in rows and columns, or a series of statistical observations

degenerate star   a star composed mostly of degenerate matter, such as a neutron star or white dwarf

deviate   a statistical distribution item that differs appreciably from the norm

Dicke-switched receiver   in physics, a type of radioastronomy receiver

Dik-dik Hill   paleological site in Olduvai Gorge, Tanzania

direct coupling in a circuit, conduction rather than induction or capacity coupling between two valve or transistor stages

directrix a line used in calculations from points on a conic section

dissipation trail a clear rift left behind a plane flying through thin cloud layers

double slit experiment a physics experiment, the directing of a stream of particles toward a screen but through two slits in an intermediary screen (more particles reach certain areas of the back screen when one of the slits is closed down)

edaphic climax an ecological climax related to soil factors

ethyl lactate a colorless water-soluble liquid ester

excited state any state of a physical system higher in energy than the ground state

explicit relation in mathematics, a functional relation in which the dependent variable is stated directly in terms of the independent variable

flagellated chamber in the central cavity of a sponge, an outpouching of a wall

Fokker-Planck equation a mathematical equation from the theory of diffusion and occurring in the theory of stochastic processes

Frenkel defect a lattice vacancy arising from removal of an ion from its site

frontal organ an organ found at the front of the head of certain crustaceans

Gay Lussac's law a law governing the thermal expansion of gases

Haller's organ a sense organ on the anterior legs of certain ticks

Hartree-Fock approximation in physics, a method for the solution of a problem involving many electrons

Hefner candle a German standard unit of luminous intensity

hemicolloid a colloid with small particles

homopause a level of transition between the homosphere and the heterosphere, where molecular oxygen begins to dissociate into atomic oxygen

homoscedastic   in statistics, having equal standard deviations

homosphere   the lower part of the atmosphere

Hooker telescope   the 100-inch telescope (1919) at Mount Wilson

horizontal intensity   the horizontal component of the earth's magnetic field intensity

horny sponge   a sponge with a horny skeleton but no spicules

hypermastigote   a type of flagellate symbiotic in the intestine of termites

induced drag   air drag of an airfoil owing to a source independent of surface friction

interstellar reddening   the reddening of light as it passes through interstellar space

irrational number   a number expressible as an infinite decimal whereby no consecutive digits repeat themselves indefinitely

kink instability   in plasma physics, a kinking or bending of a current-carrying filament in pinch-effect geometry

Kipp generator   a glass laboratory apparatus for generating a gas

Kundt tube   in physics, a glass tube used in a method for determining velocity of sound

latus rectum   in geometry, the chord of a conic section through a focus and parallel to a directrix

lecher wires   a type of transmission line used mostly for measurement of frequencies in the high radio-frequency range

Lick Observatory   an observatory (1888) on Mount Hamilton in California

long-period variable   a type of star whose fluctuating light is relatively regular and takes months or years to complete one cycle

loose coupling   a type of coupling of two electrical circuits

Lucy   skeletal remains of a female hominid found in Ethiopia in 1974

lutrine   relating to the otter

magnetic pumping   a method of heating a plasma to a very high ion temperature; also, a method of using a magnetic field to move a conducting field

matrass   a rounded glass flask with a long neck formerly used for dissolving substances

mean deviation   a mathematical deviation (of n sample values x about a point a)

menstrual epact   the number of days' difference between a lunar month and a calendar month

mesofurca   the middle apodeme of an insect's thorax

outgassing   the primordial release of gases and water from earth's interior

pelvic girdle   in the trunk of a vertebrate, the skeletal structure to which the hind limbs or pelvic fins are attached

pinch effect   a result of an electromagnetic attraction of parallel currents

Poynting theorem   the rate of electromagnetic energy transfer is proportional to the product of the electric and magnetic intensities

preclimax   a relatively stable ecological community that occurs where precipitation is less than adequate

Pump   Antlie or Air Pump, a constellation in the Southern Hemisphere near Canis Major

self-excitation   using a dynamo current to excite the dynamo's field magnets

sex-intergrade   an individual intermediate in sexual characters

sextactic   in geometry, relating to tangency at six coincident points

sextuplex   describing a particular system of telegraphy allowing six messages to be sent simultaneously over one wire

streptaster   a sponge spicule that is like a modified aster

suctorian   one of a class of protozoans

Trojan group   a group of eleven asteroids each of which has a period and mean distance very similar to those of Jupiter

two-body problem   in physics, the problem of predicting the positions and motion of two objects given certain information

vagile organism   an organism free to move about

vaginicolous   in zoology, describing certain protozoans that build a pipelike cover around themselves and live within it

vena contracta   in hydraulics, a particular contractional point in a jet of fluid

vulgar establishment   the average interval of time between the moon's upper transit and the first high water thereafter

Witch of Agnesi   a curve whose equation is $x\,y = 4a\,(2a-y)$

WHAT KIND OF TALK IS THAT? QUIZ NO. 12

In what subject or field are the following terms used?

funiculus
hirsute
latex
fleshy
volva
carbon balls
Fragrant Clitocybe
Silky Volvaria
Hairy Stereum
Dung Roundhead
Blue Leg

Cramp Balls
Velvet Shank
Naked Tricholoma
Honey Tuft
Hairy Rubber Cup
Black-Nipple Fiber
   Head
Slippery Jill
Black Jelly Roll
Slimy Lactarius
Peniophora gigantea

Answer on page 228.

Sexy Sports Line

Nowadays, in the Age of the 900 number, you can dial—and pay—for information about the weather, the time, traffic, astrology, crossword puzzle solutions, the future (as determined by psychics), medical advice, financial advice, and pro team scores. You can even telephone a properly breathy voice to provide you with aural arousal—a true party line.

When it comes to male telephone customers, sports news and erotic encouragement are probably the two most popular 900-number services. What if some enterprising entrepreneur were to combine the two? Why not make it possible for guys to get touch-tone foreplay and athletic play-by-play (a mixture of scores and scoring) at the same time? Wouldn't it go something like this?

■　■　■

Extension 1:
Hi, my name's Laura, and this is your twenty-four-hours-a-day Sports Sex Fantasy Line—the call-in phone service that lets

you guys hear the genuine sports lingo, win a prize, and get turned
on at the same time!

Say, fella, can you guess our mystery sport today?

*How do you feel about scoring on a petticoat? Are you inter-
ested in getting unstrung by a girl who knows quite a lot about
foreshafts, prick shafts, and floo-floos? I know what a good piece
of lipping is, too. I know about cock feathers. And for you, honey,
I have just the right shaft rubber!*
(Answer on page 107).

Extension 2:

Hi, my name's Dawn, and this is your twenty-four-hours-a-
day Sports Sex Fantasy Line—the call-in phone service that lets
you guys hear the genuine sports lingo, win a prize, and get turned
on at the same time!

Say, fella, can you guess our mystery sport today?

*I'm still kind of a gutter gal who knows her hooking lanes,
and with me you'll always have a big ball and some nice cheese-
cake! Do you know how to take care of a barmaid (one in the
dark)? Face a bedpost, or a spread eagle, or a Greek Church?
Tired of a flat box? Of those cherries? Of striking out? Let me
teach you a bit about the old out and in!*
(Answer on page 107.)

Extension 3:

Hi, my name's Brenda, and this is your twenty-four-hours-a-
day Sports Sex Fantasy Line—the call-in phone service that lets
you guys hear the genuine sports lingo, win a prize, and get turned
on at the same time!

Say, fella, can you guess our mystery sport today?

*Even when the big ones are humping, I don't mind a go-
behind and some fancy hot-dogging. Like to see my bottom turn?
Don't forget your baggies!*
(Answer on page 107.)

Extension 4:

Hi, my name's Rachel, and this is your twenty-four-hours-a-day Sports Sex Fantasy Line—the call-in phone service that lets you guys hear the genuine sports lingo, win a prize, and get turned on at the same time!

Say, fella, can you guess our mystery sport today?

If I try a leg attack, will I have to worry about your sprawl and crossface? Hmm, which one of us should have the position of advantage for the most fun? Can you handle a cross-buttock? A high crotch? Or are you only up to a butt-drag? Try a sitout with me, big boy, and I may show you my suckback! I know all about your go-behind. I know you'd love to be riding me, wouldn't you? If you're thinking of penetration, forget it!

(Answer below.)

Answers to "Sexy Sports Line":

Extension 1: archery
Extension 2: bowling
Extension 3: surfing
Extension 4: wrestling (nonprofessional)

WHAT KIND OF TALK IS THAT? QUIZ NO. 13
In what subject or field are the following terms used?

symbolic debugger   insertion point
greeking   string handling
swapping   soft clip area
backward chaining   nibble
explicit address   latency
hard failure   X-height

Answer on page 228.

Branded Names

Parents have been known to give their children names that are semantically unfortunate, even life-warping. In branding their products, manufacturing companies know better. Or do they?

From hardware store items to toys and candy, some brand names give one pause. A person could even be discouraged from ordering a particular product over the telephone. Over the years, these products come and go, of course. For example, we no longer see or hear about Continuous Strip patterned flooring, Big Yazoo boats, Vibrator musical reeds and mouthpieces, Screw Mate drills, Screw-Fast electric screwdrivers, Beat It dog repellent, Goose-Lite portable inspection lights, Felt-Tite typewriter pads, Potty Bear stuffed animals, Hot Pans fluorescent watercolors, Screwy Balls candy, and Cherry Humps candy bars.

But numerous other wares and comestibles bearing suggestive names are for sale at this very moment in stores across America. You can find all of them listed in the latest edition of *Brands and Their Companies,* published by Gale, which also indicates the nature of the product. Many of the entries, however, are followed by the intriguing words "product description unknown." What will we get for our hard-earned money when we buy the mysterious products sold under the names Birth Studs, Contilox, French Wash, or Snatch Pants?

Some of the product names are simply those of the company founders or owners. Others were presumably chosen in good faith, if with a certain semantic tone-deafness. Chicago Combustion Corporation, for example, produces both a Big Sixty I gas stove and a Big Sixty II gas stove. We can only wait to see what they will call their ninth model.

Here are some brand names under which various consumer goods are currently sold in the U.S. of A. Can you guess what kind of product each represents? (Answers on page 112.)

Ball Doctor	Dorko
Bare Bottoms	Fanny
Bastad	Feeling Saucy
Big Beaver (I)	Felter Fast
Big Beaver (II)	Finger Front & Back
Big Blow	French Cherry
Big Hunk	Fugbug!
Big Pumper	Hanky Panky
Boobie	Hardan
Bust-Rust	Hardman
Buttock's	Head Girls
Cheeks	Hooker
Climax	Hooter
Come Together	Hot Basket
Cont	Juggs
Coosa	Klitter Korde
Dick Held	Knocker Stocker
Diddle Cow	Longstrip
Dirty	Mini Buns
Donghia	Nipple

Nookies
Nut Zippers
Penestain
Penetrator
Pissel the Parakeet
Poopatroopers
Potty
Pussy

Putz
Silk Laid
Strip and Grip
Strip-Lay
Tinkling Twins
Titti
Whang
Whoppers

Answers to "Branded Names" Quiz:

Ball Doctor repair kit for inflatable balls (Unique Sports Products, Inc.)

Bare Bottoms women's shoes (International Seaway Trading Corp.)

Bastad shoes (Three Crown Import, Inc.)

Big Beaver brooms (Prefex Corp.)

Big Beaver potato products (Mid-American Potato Co.)

Big Blow chewing gum (Rudolph Enterprises, Inc.)

Big Hunk candy (Annabelle Candy Co., Inc.)

Big Pumper toy (Tonka Corp.)

Boobie stuffed toy (Gund, Inc.)

Bust-Rust penetrating oil (G-96 Design Tech, Inc.)

Buttock's protective ointment (Emerson Laboratories)

Cheeks men's apparel (Trend Master)

Climax tobacco (American Brands, Inc.)

Come Together greeting cards (Stanyan Record Co.)

Cont food products (Acme Foods)

Coosa men's slacks and shorts (Rome Manufacturing Co.)

Dick Held sports equipment (The Harry Gill Co.)

Diddle Cow stuffed animal (Berrie & Co., Inc.)

Dirty potato chips (Chickasaw Chips)

Donghia furniture (Donghia Furniture Co., Ltd.)

Dorko embroidery scissors (Norsk Engros USA, Inc.)

Fanny artists' brushes (Stangren, Inc.)

Feeling Saucy mushroom entrees (Monterey Mushrooms, Inc.)

Felter Fast wall construction system (Triangle Metal and Manufacturing Co.)

Finger Front & Back girdles and corsets (Coree Creations Corp.)

French Cherry soft drink (Snapple Juice & Soda)

Fugbug! insect repellent for personal use (Atomic Products Corp.)

Hanky Panky cookies (General Biscuit Co., Inc.)

Hardan sports apparel (Stem Hat & Sportswear Corp.)

Hardman   pianos (Aeolian Pianos, Inc.)
Head Girls   apparel (American Argo Corp.)
Hooker   ring toss game (Rathcon, Inc.)
Hooter   stuffed toy (Gund, Inc.)
Hot Basket   bread warmer (Salton, Inc.)
Juggs   percussion instruments and accessories (Juggs Percussion)
Klitter Korde   craft cord (Textile Enterprises, Inc.)
Knocker Stocker   toy vehicle (Mattel, Inc.)
Longstrip   plank flooring (Tarkett, Inc.)
Mini Buns   breakfast cereal (Kellogg's Company)
Nipple   rice crackers (Umeya Rice Cake Co.)
Nookies   snack food (Glenn Foods, Inc.)
Nut Zippers   candy (Squirrel Brand Co.)
Penestain   stains (Wampler Chemical Corp.)
Penetrator   toy (Tonka Corp.)
Pissel the Parakeet   bird cages (Dunigan, Opal)
Poopatroopers   toy (Imperial Toy Corp.)
Potty   tote bags (Lee's Decorating & Design)
Pussy   artists' brushes (Stangren, Inc.)
Putz   pomade (Burnishine Products, Inc.)
Silk Laid   stationery (Crane & Co., Inc.)
Strip and Grip   envelopes (New York Envelope Corp.)
Strip-Lay   self-adhesive vinyl tiles (Katz Floor Coverings Co.)
Tinkling Twins   rattles (A-Plus Products Corp.)
Titti   doll (Cardinal Industries, Inc.)
Whang   sportswear (Washington Manufacturing Co.)
Whoppers   candy (Leaf, Inc.)

WHAT KIND OF TALK IS THAT? QUIZ NO. 14
In what subject or field are the following terms used?

anal triad
sex-limited character
Skaggs Robinson
  paradox
coaxing hypnosis
F factor

gyrus fornicatus
alimentary orgasm
consentual eye reflex
anaclitic
crude score

Answer on page 228.

A.H.E.M. Animals

Just about everybody claims to like animals. But just how far will we extend ourselves for the cause of furry or feathered creatures?

Certain species of animals, some of them endangered, have peculiar names. Because their names are a little embarrassing to utter, we hear little about them. These animals are nomenclaturally disadvantaged. They are onomastically underprivileged.

Fortunately, there is an organization dedicated to their cause. It is the Animal Hospice Emergency Management Fund, or A.H.E.M. Fund. Would you be willing to be one of those manning the phones to solicit contributions for the A.H.E.M. Fund?

A.H.E.M. volunteers are asked to word their telephone appeals in the following ways to win generous pledges from people solicited.

■　■　■

Hello, Sir!

I represent the A.H.E.M. Fund for protecting sea life. Can we put you down for a contribution to save the female snapper and the bladdernose clapmatch and help a local directress to expand her small platypusary?

Hello, Ma'am!
    Like you, we at the A.H.E.M. Fund are deeply concerned about small creatures threatened with extinction. May we count on you to make a small contribution to preserve reddish South American titis and North American spermophiles?

Hello, Sir!
    I represent the A.H.E.M. Fund, and one of our priorities this year is protecting the animals of Africa. Can I put you down for a contribution to save the red-belly dik-dik, the aasvogel, Speke's pectinator, and some South African aases?

Hello, Sir!
    I'm with the A.H.E.M. Fund and hope you're having a nice day. Can we take this opportunity to call upon you for a small donation to save the hopping filanders of the Aru Islands and Asia's wild urin?

Hello, Ma'am!
    The A.H.E.M. Fund could desperately use your help to save Abbot's duiker, Anthony's pocket mouse, and Juliana's golden mole. Won't you contribute today?

Hello, Ma'am!
    I'm calling for the A.H.E.M. Fund, which tries to protect animals worldwide. Does your heart go out to the brown howler and masked titi of Brazil? Please contribute!

Hello, Sir!
    The A.H.E.M. Fund needs your help. Please aid us by reaching for your checkbook and getting behind the Spanish giant ass.

GLOSSARY

aase   the caama, a South African fox
aasvogel   a South African vulture
Abbot's duiker   a small antelope of Tanzania
Anthony's pocket mouse   a small mouse of Cedros Island, West
   Baha, California
bladdernose clapmatch   the female hooded seal
brown howler   a South American monkey
filander   a kangaroo of the Aru Islands
Juliana's golden mole   a mole of South Africa
masked titi   a Brazilian monkey
platypusary   a place for caring for or exhibiting platypuses
red-belly dik-dik   an antelope of East Africa
snapper   a snapping turtle
Spanish giant ass   a breed of donkey almost as large as the
   Poitou ass
Speke's pectinator   a bushy-tailed gundi-like animal of Somalia
   and Ethiopia
spermophile   a squirrel
titi   a small South American reddish or grayish monkey
urin   the urial, an Asian wild sheep

■   ■   ■   ■   ■   ■   ■   ■   ■

UNUTTERABLE SOUTH AMERICA!

Four-week eleven-country tour. Go south of the border where other travelers dare not go—or admit they've gone! You will visit:

Ballo, Hotzuc, Sucum, and Titzupan in Mexico
Titi in Colombia
Cuntan in Guatemala
Cum Cum and Horno in Honduras
Pis Pis Bodega and the Vulvul River in Nicaragua
Lake Titicaca in Bolivia
Sucatinga, Mamory, and Fartura in Brazil
Cuntaya Quebrada and Pusi in Peru
Punta Cock in Chile
El Hunco in Argentina

FOR DETAILS AND BOOKINGS, CONTACT GLOBE-TROTS TRAVEL
AGENCY

■   ■   ■   ■   ■   ■   ■   ■   ■

WHAT KIND OF TALK IS THAT? QUIZ NO. 15
In what subject or field are the following terms used?

anomalistic period
breakoff feeling
bleed off
damping maneuver
dose rate

goxing
leveled thrust
shedding her skirt
snort track

Answer on page 228.

His ultimate dream,
of course, was to
make a truly
stunning-looking
secretary with a
drop-front and
swing legs.

This Saturday morning Leonard was still in the bathroom working with a pet cock. He found himself thinking of a swing joint. And a real bender! Alma had given him not one but two hickeys but he couldn't remember where they were. Besides enjoying a close check of Alma's plumbing, there were the peeling hips of the jerkinhead, the breastsummer, some sweating . . .

Alma had been wonderful on the roof with that splayed skirting and eaves flashing strip. Then she had stood on the ladder and given him the shakes. Next week, she said, she wanted to learn a little about check-throating. Leonard couldn't wait. There was always the worry about her falling off the roof. But she pooh-poohed his concern that she was some delicate "period piece." Then he frowned. What if Alma really was seeing that slime, Vasco de Ferens, on the sly? Not only seeing him but harboring him right in their attic? Leonard tried not to think about it.

After making a phone call about a choke nipple, clutch diaphragm spring, box wrench, screw key, dado head, and some cheek nailing, Leonard was momentarily tired but also a little worked up. Upward and onward! He went down to his den, let go of his flaring tool, and bent over to study his latest crotch veneer. Alma preferred the feather crotch and had contributed some tung oil. There was always the possibility of impreg. He still planned to do some bodying in.

If Leonard was pleased wielding his cornering tool or examining a gland flange, for Alma it was curtains. The possibilities were endless. Fabrics! A one-piece? A sheer skirt? Or take a crepe instead? What would Leonard think about tucking it in? Whatever, she wanted something well-hung. Leonard was frequently of help, whether checking her felt valance, going for her cup hooks, or standing on a chair near the dormer waggling that swinging extension rod. He especially liked Alma's reverse French seams. Now she had to learn something about a bias strip.

Would the two of them ever finally succeed with that ceiling mounting? And Alma still had to call her close friend Sally, who

Hardcore Homebodies

An eccentric aspiring writer of recent years, Mr. Ernest Koomb, started a "novel" about a country couple, Leonard and Alma Melton, who were positively (or negatively) obsessed with their house and furniture and spent every spare minute making improvements. They were also preoccupied with a mysterious ghost in their attic. Or was it a ghost?

Mr. Koomb never got to complete *Leonard and Alma* before his early death, but we are fortunate to have his bemused family's permission to reprint its opening fragment.

According to Koomb's relatives, this bizarre narrative is quite autobiographical in that the writer himself was an avid restorer of old houses, if not of the English language. They stumbled upon the unfinished manuscript in an attic, along with many rather discouraging rejection letters from publishing houses.

Of Koomb's strange paean to tools, carpentry, and plumbing, one family member remarked that Koomb here "included everything and the kitchen sink, too, leaving out only the flat boring bit." (The flat boring bit is in fact the name of a tool.)

LEONARD AND ALMA

"Cant strip on the roof, screw furring channels, and don't forget the menstruum!"

This was only one of Alma Melton's often confused jottings and hardware shopping lists related to her weekend activities with her husband, Leonard. They had an old country place, a house of old repute—you could see the eaves dropping—and it was time for fixing up, starting with the front door. Leonard was partial to classic pear-shaped knockers and wanted a change.

This Saturday also proved to be the day they solved the mystery of the attic ghost!

"... Plug to Leonard, socket to me, AC-DC ..."

Bouncily, Alma went down to the backyard, bent over, and shook some old dirt out of her large and ample brazier. She suddenly remembered another item for her shopping list, a long nipple.

But sometimes she couldn't stop wondering about the ghost. Lately they had heard those sounds coming from up in the fireplace attic room again, low moaning sounds. It was quite scary. There were rumors that the house was haunted by the spirit of an old Scotsman who had died under mysterious circumstances. To make matters worse, Leonard was the jealous type. Alma had an old flame named Vasco de Ferens, and Leonard seemed suspicious that maybe Alma secretly had Vasco hiding somewhere in the attic. Silly man! Alma wondered if the deep, puttering sounds might not be the work of their realtor friend, Douglas Pouch, who was a practical joker and thought Leonard should "loosen up" a bit. Would they ever solve the mystery?

Back to work! Leonard didn't like to see Alma handling too many dangerous men's tools, of course. He often warned her to stay away from pinch bars and tit drills and the like. Not knowing one tool from another, they were so many dinguses to her. His spouse couldn't really differentiate between types of screws. The

eye screw, a leveling screw, the interrupted screw—silly her, one was as good as another!

But Leonard had given her something lately, and it had been a wrench! She now spent lots of time up in the old messy bathroom, where Leonard enjoyed checking out her increasingly impressive plumbing. He had coached her about static head and PP and blow bags and adjusting her new ball-check valve and diaphragm washer, and now she could do admirable things with elbows, shoulders, you name it! Alma already knew how to use penetrating oil, how to service a ball cock on the toilet, and, with a little help, could mount pretty much any new bathroom fixture, even on a pedestal. They were now looking into male transition couplings.

But her thoughts turned again to the attic ghost. Two nights ago they had heard it again. It sounded almost like an echoing, sputtering motor. Had Leonard left some old power tool up there? With a flashlight and a shotgun, he went up to explore in the middle of the night. He found nothing, of course. But back in the bedroom he made some remark about not wanting ever to catch her with Vasco de Ferens. Men!

Leonard had insisted she help him on the ladder with some upper-wall insulation, and she still had to get the felt up. Or she hoped Leonard could get it up.

"... get hidden slot screwed joint, a spreadable Molly ..."

Leonard himself was never happier than when, male hose cet or nut driver in hand, he was sizing, tonguing-and-groovin finishing. Or sheeting all over. He was inexhaustible, Alma ted to amazed friends, "no matter how much he's drilled tered." As for the latter, she had helped Leonard two w earlier and learned a little about such things as prickin avoiding unsightly blowing.

"... hook strip, stud fixing, double ball catch ..."

Back at their jobs on Monday, though, the Melton a little tired, possibly from the terminology they foun using on weekends.

Hardcore Homebodies

An eccentric aspiring writer of recent years, Mr. Ernest Koomb, started a "novel" about a country couple, Leonard and Alma Melton, who were positively (or negatively) obsessed with their house and furniture and spent every spare minute making improvements. They were also preoccupied with a mysterious ghost in their attic. Or was it a ghost?

Mr. Koomb never got to complete *Leonard and Alma* before his early death, but we are fortunate to have his bemused family's permission to reprint its opening fragment.

According to Koomb's relatives, this bizarre narrative is quite autobiographical in that the writer himself was an avid restorer of old houses, if not of the English language. They stumbled upon the unfinished manuscript in an attic, along with many rather discouraging rejection letters from publishing houses.

Of Koomb's strange paean to tools, carpentry, and plumbing, one family member remarked that Koomb here "included everything and the kitchen sink, too, leaving out only the flat boring bit." (The flat boring bit is in fact the name of a tool.)

LEONARD AND ALMA

"Cant strip on the roof, screw furring channels, and don't forget the menstruum!"

This was only one of Alma Melton's often confused jottings and hardware shopping lists related to her weekend activities with her husband, Leonard. They had an old country place, a house of old repute—you could see the eaves dropping—and it was time for fixing up, starting with the front door. Leonard was partial to classic pear-shaped knockers and wanted a change.

This Saturday also proved to be the day they solved the mystery of the attic ghost!

". . . Plug to Leonard, socket to me, AC-DC . . ."

Bouncily, Alma went down to the backyard, bent over, and shook some old dirt out of her large and ample brazier. She suddenly remembered another item for her shopping list, a long nipple.

But sometimes she couldn't stop wondering about the ghost. Lately they had heard those sounds coming from up in the fireplace attic room again, low moaning sounds. It was quite scary. There were rumors that the house was haunted by the spirit of an old Scotsman who had died under mysterious circumstances. To make matters worse, Leonard was the jealous type. Alma had an old flame named Vasco de Ferens, and Leonard seemed suspicious that maybe Alma secretly had Vasco hiding somewhere in the attic. Silly man! Alma wondered if the deep, puttering sounds might not be the work of their realtor friend, Douglas Pouch, who was a practical joker and thought Leonard should "loosen up" a bit. Would they ever solve the mystery?

Back to work! Leonard didn't like to see Alma handling too many dangerous men's tools, of course. He often warned her to stay away from pinch bars and tit drills and the like. Not knowing one tool from another, they were so many dinguses to her. His spouse couldn't really differentiate between types of screws. The eye screw, a leveling screw, the interrupted screw—silly her, one was as good as another!

But Leonard had given her something lately, and it had been a wrench! She now spent lots of time up in the old messy bathroom, where Leonard enjoyed checking out her increasingly impressive plumbing. He had coached her about static head and PP and blow bags and adjusting her new ball-check valve and diaphragm washer, and now she could do admirable things with elbows, shoulders, you name it! Alma already knew how to use penetrating oil, how to service a ball cock on the toilet, and, with a little help, could mount pretty much any new bathroom fixture, even on a pedestal. They were now looking into male transition couplings.

But her thoughts turned again to the attic ghost. Two nights ago they had heard it again. It sounded almost like an echoing, sputtering motor. Had Leonard left some old power tool up there? With a flashlight and a shotgun, he went up to explore in the middle of the night. He found nothing, of course. But back in the bedroom he made some remark about not wanting ever to catch her with Vasco de Ferens. Men!

Leonard had insisted she help him on the ladder with some upper-wall insulation, and she still had to get the felt up. Or she hoped Leonard could get it up.

"... get hidden slot screwed joint, a spreadable Molly ..."

Leonard himself was never happier than when, male hose faucet or nut driver in hand, he was sizing, tonguing-and-grooving, or finishing. Or sheeting all over. He was inexhaustible, Alma admitted to amazed friends, "no matter how much he's drilled or plastered." As for the latter, she had helped Leonard two weekends earlier and learned a little about such things as pricking up and avoiding unsightly blowing.

"... hook strip, stud fixing, double ball catch ..."

Back at their jobs on Monday, though, the Meltons always felt a little tired, possibly from the terminology they found themselves using on weekends.

This Saturday morning Leonard was still in the bathroom working with a pet cock. He found himself thinking of a swing joint. And a real bender! Alma had given him not one but two hickeys but he couldn't remember where they were. Besides enjoying a close check of Alma's plumbing, there were the peeling hips of the jerkinhead, the breastsummer, some sweating . . .

Alma had been wonderful on the roof with that splayed skirting and eaves flashing strip. Then she had stood on the ladder and given him the shakes. Next week, she said, she wanted to learn a little about check-throating. Leonard couldn't wait. There was always the worry about her falling off the roof. But she pooh-poohed his concern that she was some delicate "period piece." Then he frowned. What if Alma really was seeing that slime, Vasco de Ferens, on the sly? Not only seeing him but harboring him right in their attic? Leonard tried not to think about it.

After making a phone call about a choke nipple, clutch diaphragm spring, box wrench, screw key, dado head, and some cheek nailing, Leonard was momentarily tired but also a little worked up. Upward and onward! He went down to his den, let go of his flaring tool, and bent over to study his latest crotch veneer. Alma preferred the feather crotch and had contributed some tung oil. There was always the possibility of impreg. He still planned to do some bodying in.

If Leonard was pleased wielding his cornering tool or examining a gland flange, for Alma it was curtains. The possibilities were endless. Fabrics! A one-piece? A sheer skirt? Or take a crepe instead? What would Leonard think about tucking it in? Whatever, she wanted something well-hung. Leonard was frequently of help, whether checking her felt valance, going for her cup hooks, or standing on a chair near the dormer waggling that swinging extension rod. He especially liked Alma's reverse French seams. Now she had to learn something about a bias strip.

Would the two of them ever finally succeed with that ceiling mounting? And Alma still had to call her close friend Sally, who wanted to relocate up here and was nervous about a penetration test.

For the moment, Alma was busy sniffing an old toilet cover and thinking about Leonard's hair trunk and her bulging old chest. Should she get a flatter chest? On the side table she jerked up a fat sperm candle and lingeringly fingered the waxy pricket. Furniture! Leonard loved good old American cherry, and she couldn't wait to go to town. Later she could show him her new flush-bottom drawers.

After shaking out her ample brazier some more, Alma remembered Leonard's birthday was approaching. She'd probably surprise him with an orifice meter. He had made it quite clear he didn't want a prick punch or a six-inch tool grinder. (For her last birthday, Leonard had given her her own cramps in the garage.) At the rate Leonard was spending, she might have to become a steady bargainer beneath the golden balls!

Leonard never felt really insulated, and in the attic she found him holding his six-inch bat between two ceiling joists. Later, on the staircase he showed her his proud new riser and asked for some help with his front string before getting involved with some nosing. Leonard particularly liked nosing butts. He had also once made commode steps incredibly quickly.

After Alma herself did an admirable threshold strip in their front bedroom, when she ultimately did not go for the PG sticking, Leonard was ready for some serious nailing. Alma was not good at things like toenailing or feather-tonguing, but she tried to provide Leonard with whatever he needed, whether a headless set screw, a dog screw, or another screw starter.

While Alma drove into town, Leonard had an ax and was out at the old wood pile whacking off scores of termites. Leonard disliked termites almost as much as he disliked the cunning lyctus. Later, after crawling around looking for some loose morels, he relaxed in his garage workshop for all his vises. What surprise would his wife have in store for his birthday? Soft jaws—that was what he needed. Also, a clutch-head bit. He now had nailing tables, a tonguing board, a deep-throat clamp, and was thinking of treating himself to a Roman ogee router bit, some Trojan snips ... Also, should he and Alma put in some sort of small pond or pocket pool?

Back from town, Alma decided not to show Leonard her new flush-bottom drawers until later. Already he drooled over her fall-front drawers. He knew, too, that whenever he wedged his hand into Alma's drawers he would find lots of fragrant potpourri.

For a moment, she thought she could hear that ghostly sound again coming from the back attic room. It sounded like—like a tuneless bagpipe drone. Or something more unmentionable! She shuddered. Or had their friend Douglas Pouch, who sometimes stayed over, done something in the attic as a prank? Time to turn one's mind to other things!

From Rumpp to Coit, Alma knew her appointments. Then there was the picture she had recently seen of an exciting Wangentisch with a box stretcher. Oh, for some cock's-head hinges! Fortunately Leonard was always receptive to a new piece, and she loved moving them around! She kept thinking about that one nightstand at Ike Murphy's garage sale last week.

The first thing she did today was move her swell front. Then she neatened the rolled-up body Brussels on Leonard's old hair trunk, which seemed to have some kind of veneer disease. That disappointing sawbuck table! When they had company for a big dinner, she had to spread those heavy legs. Annoying! And that desktop was too small. Nothing like a good scrutoire to do her real communicating! And what was more exciting for a couple than a chest-on-chest?

Seats! Thank God, she'd gotten rid of her worn-out lover's chair and old womb chair. As for Leonard, he loved her open-back and split-bottom (better than that old shuck-bottom) but was less than happy when he saw the sausage turning on her love seat. Maybe one day they'd have an incredible tête-à-tête, or perhaps a vis-à-vis. Except that at an auction she'd first take a low crapaud. Leonard always said he'd prefer to see his wife on a sofa with splay legs and rollover arms. And he looked forward to one day being able to sit on a pouf.

Upstairs there was the straddle chair awaiting her husband's very own claw-and-ball feet. He had also managed a liquor cabinet with a pickled finish. She was not quite so pleased about Leonard's self-rimming vanity. Now all they needed was a clap table, maybe with cock beading. Or some old French vaisselier? Or a gout stool—maybe she could get her hands on a few stool samples. If not, Leonard was a handy craftsman.

It was late that Saturday afternoon that Leonard solved the mystery of the attic ghost—and got relieved of his suspicions of Vasco de Ferens. He was probing the old fireplace in the attic back room with a stick when he felt something wedged into the narrow flue. Out fell one of those rubber bladders known as a whoopee cushion. He called Alma upstairs. When he squeezed it, they both blushed. Obviously the work of that prankster Douglas Pouch.

Alma and Leonard both had a stiff highball to celebrate solving the mystery. No more talk of Vasco de Ferens! Leonard put away his shotgun. He was feeling especially invigorated, itching to get involved with some floor planking. Or whatever! His ultimate dream, of course, was to make a truly stunning-looking secretary with a drop-front and swing legs.

GLOSSARY

ball-check valve a type of round valve pushed by fluid pressure

bender a machine for bending parts

bias strip a strip cut on a slant or diagonally

blow bag (or expansion nozzle) an attachment (for a garden hose) used to clear drains

blowing small pits in a plaster surface because of certain material beneath that is expanding

body Brussels a Brussels carpet

bodying in in wood finishing, getting a more even finish by filling in the coarse grains

box stretcher   crossbars connecting furniture legs

box wrench   a wrench that fits completely over a nut or bolt head

brazier   a pan for burning coals

breastsummer   a wall supporting beams over a wide opening

butt   the thick end of a board, shingle, etc.

cant strip   a beveled strip used between a roof and a wall or under the lowest row of roof tiles

check-throating   a groove beneath a projecting molding that prevents rain runback

cheek nailing   a method of nailing slates, using a hole on one side of the slate and a notch on the other

chest-on-chest   one chest atop another, a seventeenth-century English furniture form; a tallboy or highboy

choke nipple   a type of pipe joint

clap table   a pier or console table of early-nineteenth-century England, usually with a looking glass

claw and ball foot   a furniture foot that resembles an animal's or bird's clasping a ball

clutch-head bit   a type of screwdriver bit

cock   any valve or faucet controlling liquid flow

cock beading   carpentry beads that project from the surface

cock's-head hinge   a hinge whose two plates are rooster's-head silhouettes

Coit   Job Coit, Jr. (1692–1741), a Boston cabinetmaker

commode step   a step with a curved front or riser

cornering tool   a cutting tool, for rounding sharp corners, whose edge is curved

coupling nut   a nut used at a pipe connection

cramp   a clamp; also, a right-angled iron bar used by masons

crapaud   an armchair that is low, wide, and heavily upholstered

crotch veneer   a thin sheet of wood, for veneering, cut at the crotch of a tree

cup hook   a hook for corners of stationary curtains

dado head   a power tool, having two circular saws, for cutting flat-bottomed grooves

deep-throat clamp   a woodworking clamp with a deep gap for clamping (a piece of wood) far from the edge

diaphragm washer   a washer used on a faucet

dingus   any thing, gadget, etc., whose name one doesn't know

dog screw   a screw with an unusual head or only half a head

drop front   a hinged cover that lowers to form a writing table, or the desk or secretary of which it is a part

elbow   an angular pipe fitting

eye screw   a screw with an eyelike head

fall-front drawer   a drawer with a front section that is hinged to fall forward

feather crotch   a feathery pattern in veneer grain

feather-tonguing   making in such a way that a tongue fits a groove

felt valence   a short drapery of felt

finish   to put a final surface or coating on

flaring tool   a tool used to flare soft metal

flashing strip   a sheet-metal strip used at the junction of a wall and roof or of two roof surfaces

flat boring bit   a spade bit used with a power drill to drill large holes

flush-bottom drawer   a drawer whose bottom is in direct contact with its support

front string   the string (or inclined side) of stairs over which the handrail goes

gland flange   a flange in an iron-body wedge gate valve

golden balls   the sign of a pawnbroker's shop

gout stool   a stool whose top is adjustable

hair trunk   a hide-covered trunk with hair not removed from the hide

headless set screw   a screw with a recessed hex head

hickey   a device used to bend pipe and conduit

hidden slot screwed joint   a joint for fastening brackets or shelves to finished work

hook strip   a wall batten on which hooks can be fastened

impreg   wood strengthened by impregnation with a resin

interrupted screw   a special screw, with sections cut out, used for a locking fit with a "mate"

jerkinhead   a hipped roof part

leveling screw   one of several adjusting screws used to make an instrument level

long nipple   a piece of pipe threaded at both ends

love seat   a settee or double chair

lover's chair   a Queen Anne–period drunkard's chair (a wide and upholstered chair)

lyctus powder-post beetle   a beetle that destroys timber

male hose faucet   a sillcock or outside faucet

male transition coupling   a type of plastic pipe fitting with external threads

menstruum   a solvent

Molly   a brand of expansion bolt

morel   a common edible mushroom

nailing tables   figures giving official nailing requirements for dwellings according to a code

nightstand   a night table

nosing   on a stair, the projection of the tread beyond the face of the riser

nut driver   a long-shank box spanner, a tool to turn smaller nuts or self-tapping screws rapidly

open-back   a chair with an unupholstered opening

orifice meter   a type of gas meter

pear-shaped knocker   a door knocker having a pear shape

pedestal   a supporting upright base

penetrating oil   oil to loosen up resistant or rusted nuts or fittings

penetration test   an on-site test (using a penetrometer) to determine the load-bearing capacity of a soil

pet cock   a small faucet, cock, or valve in a water pipe or pump to let air out

PG sticking   an unusual molding groove pattern sometimes used on window and door stiles

pickled finish   a whitish patina on furniture

pinch bar   a lever used to roll heavy wheels

pouf   an upholstered, usually round stool

PP   polypropylene (pipe for drainpipes and traps)

pricket   a candlestick with a spike, or such a spike that projects beyond the rim

pricking up   the deliberate scratching of a first coat of plaster to create the rough surface, or key, useful for another coat

prick punch   a pointed steel punch for marking or making holes in sheet metal

reverse French seam   a type of seam used instead of welting or trimming

riser   the upright part between stair treads

rollover arm   an upholstered chair arm that sweeps boldly from the side seat rails

Roman ogee router bit   a high-speed, plate-mounted motor to round off edges, cut grooves, make moldings, etc.

Rumpp   Johannel Rumpp (active c. 1740), a German designer of baroque furniture

sausage turning   a wood turning resembling sausage links

sawbuck table   a simple seventeenth-century tabletop that rests on trestles

screw furring channel   a channel used between masonry walls and plasterboard

screw key   a wrench for turning a screw or a nut

screw starter   a type of awl

scrutoire   a writing desk

secretary   a writing desk; escritoire

self-rimming vanity   a vanity with a sink rim that overlaps the counter surface and rests on it

shake   a shingle split from a log

sheer skirt   a hanging facing or flap of fabric that is diaphanous

sheeting   a film of material, such as plastic

shoulder   any part or piece serving as an abutting projection

shuck bottom   a chair with a seat made of maize husks

six-inch bat   loose-wool insulation in six-inch lengths

six-inch tool grinder   a sharpener, with a coolant pot over the grinding wheel, for edge tools

sizing   gluey material for filling pores in various surfaces

soft jaws   lead or copper covers used over the jaws of a vise to prevent damage to materials

sperm candle   a candle made of spermaceti

splay legs   legs that flare or angle outward

splayed skirting   a roof skirting having a bevel along the top edge

split bottom   having a seat made of splits

static head   a water column height that, at rest, produces a given pressure

straddle chair   a chair with a narrow back, attached shelf, and short and high arms, so that one sits facing the shelf (also called boyelle, reading chair, and cockfight chair)

stud fixing   a metal pin or bolt insertable in a surface as a fastener to facilitate further work

sweating   a kind of soldering

swell front   a cabinet or credenza having a bow or segmental front

swinging extension rod   a curtain or drapery rod that swings out to allow access to a window

swing joint   a pipe joint whose parts are movable or rotatable

swing leg   a leg (supporting a drop leaf) at the end of a hinged rail

tête-à-tête   an S-curved two-person sofa; Siamoise

threshold strip   a doorway molding

tit drill   a flat drill with a central "teat" for counterboring holes

toenailing   driving in a nail at a slant so that it can penetrate a second piece of wood

toilet cover   a cloth spread for a dressing table; toilet cloth

tongue-and-groove   to prepare boards for joining by working a groove on one edge and a ridge (or tongue) on another

tonguing board a groove-fitting device for holding a narrow piece of thin material to be planed

Trojan snips cutters for sheet metal

tung oil drying oil derived from tung tree seeds

vaisselier an eighteenth-century French dresser

vis-à-vis a nineteenth-century S-shaped double-seat chair or sofa

Wangentisch a German Renaissance furniture form circa 1500, typically a splayed-leg table with a low box stretcher

womb chair a curved and enclosing upholstered plastic chair designed by Eero Saarinen

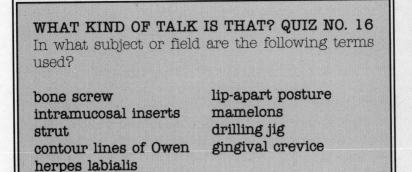

WHAT KIND OF TALK IS THAT? QUIZ NO. 16
In what subject or field are the following terms used?

bone screw
intramucosal inserts
strut
contour lines of Owen
herpes labialis

lip-apart posture
mamelons
drilling jig
gingival crevice

Answer on page 228.

Lively
Dead English

When you come upon some of the old and rare words that English speakers have used in times past, you get a definite sense that our English and American forebears were a pretty bawdy lot.

Here, flushed out of some fat and dusty dictionaries, are some of the more provocative-sounding (yet perfectly innocent) words from days gone by.

■   ■   ■

adulterine adulterated (drug); illegal; born of adultery
ambivert a person intermediate between an introvert and extrovert
anti-orgastic sedative
asinus ad lyrum one with little artistic talent or appreciation
assation baking or roasting
assestrix a female assistant
assything compensation or reparations

balductum   curdled milk; buttermilk
bastern   a sedan chair
bawcock   a fine fellow
bellibone   a fair maid
blowess   a beggar's wench; a trull
bopeeper   a mask
bounce-Jane   a delicious dish in fifteenth-century cookery
bowels   feelings of pity or compassion

cacafuego   a swaggering braggart
clinchpoop   a person lacking gentlemanly breeding
clit   (dialect) heavy, doughy, caked, sticky
clogdogdo   a made-up word, or so-called nonce word, of uncertain meaning
cockapert   impudent
cockarouse   a person of consequence
cockbrain   a giddy or rash person
cockshut   (dialect) twilight
coction   digestion of food; a phase of disease or healing
constuprate   to ravish
crotcheteer   a person with a peculiarity
cunctator   a delayer or procrastinator
cunctipotent   all-powerful; omnipotent

dimbox   a mediator

fardry   painting one's face white
farture   stuffing
fellowfeel   to sympathize with
fill-dyke   February
focage   hearth money, a tax upon one's hearth fire
forficulate   shaped like a small pair of scissors
fouter   something of little value, or "a fig"
frigefact   to chill
fucatory   counterfeit or deceitful

fucus   a cosmetic or coloring for the face
fuk   a kind of sail

gism   a fusing or joining substance, or flux

hamesucken   assaulting a person in his own home
horary   relating to an hour or hours
horry   (dialect) disgusting or foul

insessed   inhabited or dwelt in or possessed by
intitulate   to entitle

juggins   a dupe or simpleton

karnel   a kernel
kinker   an acrobat

lip-clap   kissing
liripoop   a medieval graduate's hood; a trick; a silly ass
lobcock   (dialect) a stupid, blundering person
lusthouse   an inn

manurance   the cultivation of land; cultivation or training of the
   mind
meacock   a cowardly or effeminate man
molestful   troublesome or annoying

nudiostertian   pertaining to the day before yesterday

orgulous   proud or haughty; showy or splendid

paranymph   a best man; a bridesmaid
penile   peninsular
Peter Funk   a swindler

peterman a fisherman
poop-noddy a cheater, swindler, or duper
pootly-nautch a children's puppet show
potty-baker a potter
prick and praise the highest praise
pudendous shameful

quakebuttock a coward

randy to canvass
ripesuck a person easily bribed

scruze to squeeze
scumber dog excrement
sexagesm one-sixtieth
sexcuple, sextiply to multiply by six
sextry a sacristy
shiterow a heron
shittle not constant or stable
smellfungus a fault-finder; a captious critic
spermophobe one averse to germs
spital, spittle a charity hospital

titivil a rascal or scoundrel
tongue-bang to scold
tonguefencer an arguer or debater

underfong to receive or come to have
urinator a diver

voider something which keeps things off or away, as a screen or
  piece of armor, especially a small piece over an unprotected elbow, knee, etc.
volva a female Norse soothsayer

wangateur a voodoo conjurer
wanger a pillow
wong a field or meadow

WHAT KIND OF TALK IS THAT? QUIZ NO. 17
In what subject or field are the following terms
used?

impure mate   fegatello attack
cruising range   French defense
inverted opening   orang-utan opening
fringe piece   variations
protection   Lucena's mate

Answer on page 228.

Medical Name-Dropping

The history of medicine reveals that many gifted and pioneering physicians were honored by having various anatomical parts or medical procedures named after them.

Among hundreds of such eponymous terms, those listed below are definitely the most important. Learn the names of these body parts and procedures well so that you will be comfortable conversing with physicians or impressing others at cocktail parties.

Anel's method
Assmann focus
Ball's operation
Bang's method
canal of Nuck
Coiter's muscle
Dick test
Gasser's syndrome
Hampton hump

Heine's operation
Kock pouch
Kuhnt's spaces
Lust's phenomenon
Pyle's disease
Smellie's method
strip area of Hines
Wang's test

GLOSSARY

Anel's method   the ligation of an artery above and below an aneurysm prior to an incision into and emptying of the sac

Assmann focus   the early exudative lesion of pulmonary tuberculosis

Ball's operation   the division of the sensory nerve trunks that supply the anus (for relief of pruritus ani)

Bang's method   an estimation of quantity of sugar, urea, albumin, etc., in the blood by examining a few drops on blotting paper

canal of Nuck   a vaginal process of the peritoneum

Coiter's muscle   the musculus corrugator supercilii

Dick test   an intracutaneous test of susceptibility to a toxin responsible for aspects of scarlet fever (also called Dick method)

Gasser's syndrome   hemolytic-uremic syndrome

Hampton hump   a pleura-based density seen in pulmonary infarct

Heine's operation   cyclodialysis

Kock pouch   a continent ileostomy with a reservoir and a valved opening fashioned from doubled loops of ileum

Kuhnt's spaces   shallow recesses near the posterior chamber of the eye

Lust's phenomenon   abduction with dorsal flexion on the foot, on tapping the external popliteal nerve just below the head of the fibula; indicates spasmophilia

Pyle's disease   metaphyseal dysplasia

Smellie's method   in obstetrics, delivery of the aftercoming head with the body of the child resting on the forearm of the obstetrician

strip area of Hines   the strip of cortex between motor and premotor areas

Wang's test   a quantitative test for indican

Quail-tracker Pete hoped to get his hands on a good pair of English hooters, and still remembers once being flat-footed between two thick-knees in Australia

Bird Brains and Fishy Talk

What better place for guys to glory in complete freedom of speech than the traditional American rod and gun club?

Or a bird and fish club, such as the large and active Looker and Hookers Club, in the Midwest, which attracts not only ga shooters and anglers but more pacific birders, armed only with oculars. Here is a fraternal haven where the hunters can get a from the gatherers to enjoy some fowl language and cheep t or take a healthy piscifaunal view of life.

The men belonging to Lookers and Hookers are not m cals. Most of the club's game hunters, birders, and fisherr well traveled, as club secretary Bill Shafer reports each r his minutes. We were able to acquire a photocopy of Shafer's record of a recent meeting.

MINUTES

Lookers and Hookers Club
President: Arnie Kaller
Vice President: Steve Topp
Treasurer: Doug Billings
Secretary: Bill Shafer

The last meeting of Lookers and Hookers was held on the evening of May 14 at the club's headquarters at 211 Willamette Road. Thirty-eight members were present. President Arnie Kaller called the meeting to order at 7:40 p.m.

A sense of anticipation was in the air, as the meeting was to culminate in the announcement by Arnie Kaller of the winner in our annual L & H Lottery drawing. The winning member receives a cash prize of $500.

Our president welcomed two new anglers, Pete Cohen and Ed Burnovsky, to our tweet-and-glub-glub club, with a nice little tribute touching upon the joys of the best nymphs, the bulging rise, the pickup, stripping lines, and the improved clinch. Arnie also touched upon the three-way swivel, the hump shank, the Norman Flasher, Humpies, Wood Pussies, bottom bouncing, and piddle-fishing.

Ten minutes into the meeting, member Burr Savarilis made a motion that we adjourn. Nobody seconded the motion.

The primary old business discussed was replacing the smelly old stuffed kaka and pukeko stolen from the clubhouse two months ago. Gene Lally is already looking into replacing the missing plaque to Bob Wright's prizewinning flower-pecker, but everybody agrees the great bustard that finally rotted is probably gone forever.

The question of admitting women to the club was again raised and shot down—or reeled in! Not that we don't all know one or two fine women. Like Betty Gillick down the road, who is a fantastic fly dresser and charges little. But Wilbur Allan pointed out that most females wouldn't know your wrasse from your broadtail,

WHAT KIND OF TALK IS THAT? QUIZ NO. 18
In what subject or field are the following terms used?

brown-lined labido   Geisha-girl medaka
African scat   merry widow
Duncker's barb   sucking loach
black-chinned   oral gestation
  mouthbreeder

Answer on page 228.

or a pair of healthy boobies from a nuthatch, or a fine red cock from a good Dorking. Does any club member's wife really appreciate a promising wet fly? Or the taste of butter-smeared butts or the bastard-margaret? It was agreed that, women or no women, all club members should be treated equally. No comparing of members is to be tolerated.

The anglers' annual April outing to western river regions was a great success. The party of fourteen landed many redmouths and big lip suckers as well as a few chiselmouths. Much merriment was had around the bonfire. Our favorite braggart, Joe Whitson, reportedly regaled all with Florida tales of how his skillful rod once conquered openmouthed French grunts, West Indian hump-grunts, nursehounds, smallmouths, Mexican snappers, and regular maneaters. During the outing, Joe and Vince Tofutti also did some successful jacking, off in the woods somewhere.

A little birder also told me that Sam Schultz made the mistake of letting a stray bitch into his boat one morning, and it seems she got most of her new master's bait!

Burr Savarilis again made a motion that the meeting be adjourned. It was greeted by silence. We all know Burr's favorite television program is on tonight and he resents our having meetings on Wednesdays.

Bob Soames and Ted Seligman, of the club's proud birdwatching contingent, reported on their recent extensive trip to Europe. Besides gorcocks and flycatchers, they encountered long tongues, nutjobbers, and peesweeps. Other members drooled over Bob and Ted's excellent pictures of twit-twats, blue tits, and bottle tits. Ted, who once shared with us his exciting Polaroids of chuck-will's-widow, even got a graphic shot of a figpecker with a nightjar.

Even at sea or around ducks our boys never stopped "scoping," feasting their eyes on cockawees and sea titlings, and very much enjoying the occasional laughing goose. (Ted remains curious about the Chinese goose.) Word is Bob kept crying out "Frigate!" (a premature ejaculation, as he saw no such comely birds).

And Bob once got within grabbing distance of two blue-faced boobies. Ted briefly got over to Africa, where he encountered sizable oxpeckers. He also took a night-variety shite-poke in a clapnest and is sure he "made" a boubou.

Bob and Ted's trip was so successful that our "fishy" club members are planning a trip next spring to Australia, New Zealand, and some of the Pacific islands. Everybody's eager to get firsthand experience of cockschnappers and the Samoan pusi and do a little groping for groupers. Only around Hawaii can a good rodsman get humuhumunukunukuapuaa! And why not some exciting flashers, snotgalls, titfishes, ganggangs, kakawahies, and kissing gouramis, too?

Game birds, as we all know, are the special interest of four or five of our membership. Tired of the local "barnyard chicks and gobblers," Pete Blount brought along his fowling piece last month when he visited a friend in England. Quail-tracker Pete hoped to get his hands on a good pair of English hooters, and still remembers once being flat-footed between two thick-knees in Australia. He bagged and photographed two barrel tits to go with the picture of his displaying sage cock that we all hear so much about. Word is that Pete was also keeping his hand in socially with a local goosegirl. Turned out she was married to a cockmaster!

At the meeting, President Arnie Kaller also presented our annual Naturalist Achievement Award to the L & H member showing demonstrable scientific interest in birds or fishes. This year it was presented to birder Mike Gold. Mike has plans one day to mount a squatarole. And, with his biological smarts, he is also crackers about his research on blackcocks, harder's gland, underparts, rectrices, and rictal bristles. Last year Gene Corey won for his investigations of melon-blubber.

The club's annual Wildlife Photo Contest was announced in local newspapers last month, and entries have started to come in. There are even some from local celebrities! I'm told there's one from Assemblyman Bob Kelnick with two tit-babblers. Even the wealthy lady heading our local Planned Parenthood chapter, who knows how to use a studbook, sent in a curious shot of a wet petchary in the rain.

Burr Savarilis again spoke up that we should adjourn. This time he was greeted by several dirty looks and hisses, then some mutterings. It was proposed that Burr be expelled from Lookers and Hookers. The motion was seconded and unanimously approved and Burr was escorted out.

Several members urged that we again invite a knowledgeable foreign guest to visit and give us a slide show. This time it would be for our rod wavers. Everybody enjoyed the talk in November by expert birder Ron Wapping, who came all the way from Devon, England, to teach us a bit about British game and their special terminology. Ron first talked about varying shapes of peckers. Then his slides of penduline tits, white rumps, teasers, cow clits, cherry choppers, dykies, horny wicks, juggy wrens, quick-me-dicks, pee birds, char cocks, and the old flapping windfucker knocked our socks off. You know, those English certainly know how to tell it like it is!

Several of our dangling-angling members proposed that we post some photos of colorful Caribbean and South American wet ones on the walls of the main club room. These would supplement our fine-feathered prints of redheads. Carl Ramos suggested we definitely want some views of slippery dicks here, and lane snappers and tasty bangs. We may also purchase a blowup of the voracious Indian goonch and of a few Northern Atlantic desirables, such as the mykiss and goosander of Kamchatka. All Ernie Wells can talk about is the dimensions of his 1987 mackerel cock!

Locally, our rod-wielding members have reported some good catches, including hornyheads and stumpknockers.

In our neighboring county, Jake Tooney wanted to grab bass and ended up taking a black crappie in Pine Creek. Jake reported he hopes to get back to New England to get his mouth on some tasty alewife and cunner.

An old club argument was also settled at the meeting. The

bird seen in Agnes Wilson's yard last year was no brown thrasher. It was not turdoid.

The meeting closed with the exciting announcement of the winner of the L & H Lottery by Arnie Kaller, whose lips were sealed until tonight! Arnie was distressed to announce that the winner was Burr Savarilis. We got Burr on the telephone. He agreed to rejoin the club but only if we changed our meeting night. This will be the first order of business at our next meeting.

GLOSSARY

alewife   an edible herring abundant along the Atlantic Coast
bang   a Caribbean sardine
barrel tit   another name for the bottle tit
bastard-margaret   the sailor's-choice, a small porgy
big-lip sucker   a large Columbia River basin sucker (a thick-lipped freshwater fish related to the carp)
bitch   a female dog
blackcock   the male black grouse
black crappie   the calico bass, a common sunfish
blue-faced booby   a tropical white gannet (a kind of fish-eating seabird)
blue tit   a widely distributed European titmouse
booby   a tropical sea gannet
bottle tit   the long-tailed tit, a small titmouse
bottom bouncing   a boat-fishing technique that entails repeated bouncing of a lure or sinker on the bottom
boubou   any of several African shrikes
broadtail   an Australian parrot
brown thrasher   a common long-tailed, thrushlike bird of the eastern United States
bulging rise   the resultant surface bulge when a fish takes a fly or nymph just beneath the water's surface
butt   a flatfish, especially the halibut

harder's gland   an ancillary lacrimal gland of birds and reptiles

hooter   any bird, such as an owl, with a hooting call

hornyhead   the common chub (a freshwater fish)

horny wick   a Cornwall name for the lapwing

hump-grunt   a grunter (bird) of the West Indies

hump shank   a fishing hook used in wooden, cork, or plastic lure bodies

Humpy   a hair-bodied dry fly that floats well

humuhumunukunukuapuaa   a small Hawaiian triggerfish

improved clinch   a knot much used in freshwater fishing, as to tie lures onto a line

jacking   hunting or fishing with a flashlight or other artificial light

juggy wren   a Surrey (England) name for the wren

kaka   an olive-brown parrot, with red patches, of New Zealand

kakawahie   a bright red flower-pecker

kissing gourami   a whitish labyrinth fish of southeastern Asia

lane snapper   a small snapper found from Florida to northern Brazil

laughing goose   the white-fronted goose, grayish brown with a white forehead

long tongue   the wryneck, a woodpecker with soft tail feathers

mackerel cock   the Manx shearwater, a small black and white fish

maneater   a man-eating shark

melon-blubber   a rounded fleshy mass on the heads of blackfish and related cetaceans

Mexican snapper   the red snapper

mykiss   a salmon of Kamchatka

nightjar   a common grayish brown nocturnal bird of Europe

Norman Flasher   a type of vibrating or rattling sonic plug used as a fishing lure

nursehound   the European dogfish

nuthatch   a small, long-billed, tree-climbing bird

nutjobber   a nuthatch

char cock a Northern England name for the mistle t
Cheshire, called the sad cock

cherry chopper a Worcestershire (England) name for the
flycatcher

Chinese goose a large wild goose of Asia

chiselmouth a Columbia River fish having in each jaw
horny plate

chuck-will's-widow a southern U.S. goatsucker (a type o
turnal bird) larger than the whippoorwill

clapnest an enclosure or net for capturing water birds or
that nest on the ground

cockawee the common sea duck or old squaw

cockmaster one who breeds or trains gamecocks

cockschnapper a snapper of Australia and New Zealand

common sucker the white sucker fish, used for canning

cow clit an English name for the yellow wagtail or cowbird

cunner either of two wrasses (a kind of food fish), of New E
gland or England

Dorking a large English domestic fowl

dykie a Scottish name for the hedge sparrow

figpecker a European songbird

flasher a large edible marine fish

flower-pecker a short-tailed passerine bird that feeds on insects
and mistletoe berries

flycatcher any of numerous birds that feed on insects on the
wing

fly dresser one who makes artificial flies for anglers

frigate bird a powerful raptor seabird

ganggang a small cockatoo of Australia and Tasmania

goonch a large Indian freshwater fish

goosander the common merganser of the Northern Hemisphere

goosegirl a female who tends geese

gorcock the male red grouse

great bustard a very large European land bird

grouper any of various tropical and subtropical sea basses

nymph an artificial fly (wet or dry)

openmouthed French grunt a tropical marine fish of Florida and the West Indies

oxpecker either of two starlinglike birds of Africa

pecker a bird's bill

pee bird a Surrey name for the wryneck

peesweep the lapwing

penduline tit a titmouse that constructs a hanging nest

petchary the gray kingbird

pickup an initial phase of fly-rod casting

piddle-fishing (or dapping) a stealthy style of fishing that involves sneaking up close to the fishing bank, extending the rod, and letting the fly float a foot or so before quietly lifting it up

piscifaunal pertaining to fishes of a region

pukeko a handsome water-hen or gallinule of Australia and New Zealand

quick-me-dick an Oxfordshire (England) name for the quail

rectrice the quill feathers of a bird's tail, important in controlling the direction of flight

red cock the male red grouse

redhead a diving duck of medium size

redmouth any of several grunts whose mouth is red or pink

rictal bristle a feather that grows from the base of a bird's bill

sage cock the male sage grouse

sea titling the rock pipit, a European shorebird

shite-poke any of various herons

slippery dick a small bright-colored wrasse of the western Atlantic

snotgall a carangid, marine fish (narrow-bodied with a widely forked tail) of Tasmania

squaterole the black-bellied plover

stripping lines a way of pulling fishing lines back for extra power

studbook a pedigree register of animals, especially horses

stumpknocker a small sunfish with brown speckles

teaser   an English northeast-coast name for the Arctic skua bird

thick-knee   the stone curlew, a large, long-legged plover with three toes

three-way swivel   a fishing swivel with three eyes for the fishing line

tit babbler   any of various small birds of Asia and the East Indies

titfish   the trepang of Australia and the East Indies

turdoid   like a thrush

twit-twat   the house sparrow

underpart   a part on a bird's ventral side

wet fly   an artificial fly for luring fish below the water's surface

white rump   a Northumbrian and Cumberland (England) name for the wheatear, a small bird

windfucker   an obsolete English name for the kestrel

Wood Pussy   a type of pattern used in making a freshwater bucktail fly (good for catching Pacific Coast salmon)

wrasse   any of various marine spiny-finned fishes

WHAT KIND OF TALK IS THAT? QUIZ NO. 19
In what subject or field are the following terms
used?

touch piece   debasement
androcephalous   bust type
pièce de plaisir   dump
bungtown   pistareen
plug   sweating
Valentine numbers

Answer on page 228.

■　　■　　　■　　■　　　■　　　■　　　■　　　■　　■

UNSHY SHIRES OF ENGLAND!

Four weeks' gallivanting to places in England's counties so exciting we'll have you dropping in the Isles. Send cards to all your friends with postmarks to be treasured forever! You will visit:

Itchen Stoke and Spithead in Hampshire
Piddledown Common, Studland, and Didlington in
  Dorset
Maidenhead in Berkshire
Organ Ho and Craven Arms Diddlebury in Salop
Clitsome Farm in Somersetshire
Snatch Ho in Avon
Jock's Pike in Northumberland
Bottom Flash and Hooterhall in Cheshire
Head Dike in Lincolnshire
Ball Rock, Ballsaddle Rock, and Lickham Bottom in
  Devonshire
The Rump and Scroo in Shetland
Shittlehope, Whorlands, and Rape Barn in Durham
Prickwillow and Tit Brook in Cambridgeshire
Cockintake and Lickshead in Staffordshire
Dorking in Surrey
Long Itchington in Warwickshire
Buttock in Lancashire
Fanny's Grove in Nottinghamshire

Rumps Point, Brown Queen, Hor Point, and
Tinkler's Hill in Cornwall and Isles of Scilly
Head Down on the Isle of Wight
Stud Ho in Greater London
Lower Parting in Gloucestershire
Titty Hill in West Sussex
Sittinglow in Derbyshire
Shellow Bowells in Essex
Pettings in Kent
Piddle Brook, Suckley, Lickey End, and Knockerhill
Farm in Hereford and Worcester
Barf End, Dicken-Dyke, and Dicken-Nook in North
Yorkshire
Cock Beck, Pudsey, Keighley Laycock, and Dick
Slack in West Yorkshire
Cockermouth, Cuns Fell, Whangs, Tongue Head,
Rape Haw, Carlisle Heads Nook, and Slosh in
Cumbria

FOR DETAILS AND BOOKINGS, CONTACT GLOBE-TROTS TRAVEL
AGENCY

■   ■   ■   ■   ■   ■   ■   ■   ■

Who wants quoits interrupted?

Slippery English

Scholarly research on the subject of pseudo-risqué terms in English is scant. But at a recent convention of the Modern Language Association, we were fortunate to hear a controversial paper on the subject by a Professor Conran Tallion, "Amphibology and Post-Delphic Utterance."

Professor Tallion, who is Albanian-born, has been in the vanguard of the new literary movement known as recapitulationism. To recapitulationists, the only valid purpose of all language consists in making a simple, primary assertion and then restating or rephrasing it endlessly. They also believe that the best English is that which reads like a bad translation. For the recapitulationist, poor syntax is "original synjunction" and strained or tedious metaphors are "tropish variations."

Conran Tallion's MLA lecture drew mixed reviews and traded punches, and seven attendees (six of whom had tenure) were taken to the local hospital. Certain critics of Tallion have called his recapitulationist credo bunkum, hokum, or "battological twaddle." But recapitulationism seems to be a growing movement in American academia, and one colleague has called his MLA address on banana-peel semantics "autologically notable, ever epitomizing what it so forcefully adumbrates."

With his permission, and in the interests of scholarship, we're pleased to reprint in full here Tallion's seminal speech on slippery English.

AMPHIBOLOGY AND POST-DELPHIC UTTERANCE

Certain language, even when it completely lacks full frontal crudity, can rub the wrong way and arouse quite a lot of dry humphing.

Choose the wrong English words, or arrange them in compromising positions, and you can easily be misunderstood or even violently grabbed by the nuts and troublemakers of the world. It's no fun dealing with chronic crabs, much less with irate group sects. Verbal gaffes can seem as embarrassing as regrettable sexdigitism, but without a dictionary at hand you can't just whip it out. So you get morasses of misunderstanding and can feel like a butt of jokes. It's hard not to feel a real ass in the situation.

Alas, this is not an infrequent occurrence. Without well-developed figures at hand, we can't be too censual here, but truth be told, Sol ne'er goes down on Gaia without many people getting into trouble orally—what has come upon them?—because of some untoward ejaculation. Embarrassment is no fun, and nobody, from *Homo erectus* on, has ever enjoyed exposing himself.

Double entendres and unforeseen connotations can materialize like, for example, some stage-struck intruder in a play who finds a rear entry and then is, too late, caught in the act. (To meet some actress properly, he'd need only a production schedule to look up her dress rehearsal.)

Even among practicing homoglots or committed pedagogues, certain innocently meant words and phrases can have a frigorific effect. This is simply because they look or sound—tit for tat, as it were—like similar words that are naughty. Or because the particular word or phrase can have more than one meaning. Egregious polysemy, that kind of multiple-partner signification, is not yet a crime, but sometimes one wonders whether it should be.

It's almost as if certain sentences can't help running into semantic accidents. You'll find notable boners arising in interlingual activity between, not only Joe Blow or the working stiff, but even the most cunning linguists. You can't see them coming, any more than, say, in a backseat you could make out, like a trooper with a flasher, all the road ahead. You find yourself "strapped" onto some utterance of yours that's taken a bad turn, and you'd dearly love to pull yourself off. You're embarked on dangerously slippery intercourse, but you can't withdraw in time.

Studying the oral sciences—all about French liaisons, bilabial fricatives, the uvula, the diaphragm, guttural talk—is no guarantee against such mishaps. Neither is being a punctuation expert, knowing commas or when or where you have your period or when to insert a colon. Nor will being literary help; it doesn't matter a lick whether you're an expert in French lays or a Gallic conte lover.

With our communicative tongue, then, it's as if somebody at some point committed a form of adulteration. An English language completely free of promiscuous associations is, alas, a desire not to be consummated, the empty proposition of a hopeless nympholept; and it would take a master abator to put a stop to such inadvertencies. Which is to say, to call English "the One-Meaning-Only Tongue" and "the Safe Language" would, unfortunately, be a whopping pair of titular boo-boos, the purest pap—a complete bust! If anything, its connotations are overdeveloped. Yet our given vocabulary, though tainted, is never dull; or, paradoxically, though it's somewhat flyblown, it's certainly zippy!

The problem is, few people are bright enough to realize the dangers in handling a risky, prickly word. No penetration! This is true orally as well as in books or magazines (although, in the case of monthlies, where a major, well-known organ is concerned, they may just take it out if some kind of palliating insert isn't satisfactory). But to go all the way and attempt to get rid of or "evict" such tricky vocables, to dicker to get some big cockamamie "action," as through some unnatural act of Congress—surely this would be a premature ejection. As the good book says, we shouldn't kick against the pricks.

For our language to be more regular, we'd have to have some kind of movement. We have a spunky but confusing vernacular. We're perhaps like disoriented pilots desperately roger-ing; or, you might say, like rabid lucubrators grasping at the crotchets of our tongue.

Any word is but a putative functor doing its seminal job. But there is, unfortunately, no reliable prophylactic against the pure erraticism of double meanings. You can try to avoid them, of course, by mastering a kind of prickly circumscription. But then it can appear that the person speaking or writing is wantonly distributing conundrums. No, any seeming protection is like a rubber check. Let somebody unwittingly give tongue to a pregnant locution while trying to make a sally, and it's as if a pipe-smoking dastard has whipped out his flocculent mundungus and fugged the whole room. Or as if some tippling sexagesimal's anile intrusions have suddenly become too crapulous for everybody.

Or possibly like playing a tense game of chess on a fragile table—and some titubator knocks off a piece.

Similes fail! How else to put it to you? What position to take?

Let a dose of loaded language rub up against you and don't be surprised at the afterclap or, in a crowd, mass acerbation, possibly in petto. All forms of socializing, whether idle joint mooning, eager feeling out, or more serious intercourse a posteriori, will come to a halt. Such treacherous English becomes like some foreign currency, and your average, innocent American can suddenly feel as at a loss as (yet another simile!) a Japanese in Vietnam, who wants to shoot his wad and doesn't care what he's outlaid, with much yen but no negotiable dong. He'd rather be greeted in Hawaii with a lei!

These words never cease to amaze. "*What* did she say?" It's a good guess you didn't mishear; when you're consternated, trust the suppository. Admittedly, not all people blush or get embarrassed in these loose-tongued times. One wonders whether anybody flushes anymore.

And this is only one piece of the tale. These inescapable double meanings can also be a bad influence on children, and strain relations between their parents. The youngsters sometimes catch on to the taboo meaning. In no time Mr. Smith's John is overflowing with dangerous talk. And then, even if Mrs. Jones's not put out, Mr. Jones may not let John play with his Peter.

Or communication can be seen as a game: You don't want unintended meanings to stop the action or the play. For instance, take craps. You don't appreciate distractions. Or quoits. Who wants quoits interrupted? Or, in Chicago, when you're trying to take tricks with a partner, you don't want a long wait to see who wins the rubber.

Alas, we are all the impubic heirs of an ambiguous tongue. Neither titters nor breastbeating is the answer, nor can there be any false ease. There are no easy answers, and it would be a mistake to let such hopes whet dreams of a totally "unslippery" English language. We just have to keep groping as best we can and, rather than get down, try to feel up!

Exactly which words are suggestive? Which are not? To date, scholarship is scant here. There is no super codex on the subject to get absorbed in, much less a means of semantic mensuration for the ever heavy flow of double meanings. Possibly this modest paper will serve as a wee, wee pis aller, yet one of the first water; if not exactly up everyone's alley, up yours, hopefully.

Thus it seems we can never quite separate words from secondary meanings or tainted associations. Words and significations have always had a close relationship. And, what else would you expect, they're still having relations. So let us boldly make out as best we can, maybe look on words as being merely for play!

GLOSSARY

acerbation irritation or exacerbation
amphibology grammatical ambiguity
anile old-womanish or senile
autological self-descriptive
battological repetitious (verbally)
bilabial (a sound) made using both lips
censual pertaining to a census
Chicago four-deal or club bridge
codex an early, booklike form of manuscript
consternated amazed or exasperated
conte a tale or long short story
conundrum a riddle whose answer involved a pun, or any riddle
diaphragm a tissue partition between the chest and the cavities of the abdomen
dong the currency of Vietnam
flocculent fluffy or like wool
fricative a consonant (such as *f, sh* or *th*) pronounced anatomically in a certain way
frigorific making cold or chilling
fug to make stuffy or odorous
Gaia Earth
guttural uttered or articulated in the throat
homoglot one who speaks the same language
impubic immature
in petto secretly
lucubrate to study laboriously
mensuration measurement
mundungus foul-smelling tobacco
nympholept one who longs for an unattainable ideal
pedagogue a teacher
pis aller a last recourse or expedient
polysemy a word's having more than one meaning
sexagesimal sexagenarian

sexdigitism having six fingers rather than five
Sol the sun
suppository supposititious or hypothetical
titubator a person who is reeling or stumbling
uvula a fleshy lobe that is part of the soft palate
vocable a word in terms of its letter or sounds rather than its
  meaning
yen the currency of Japan

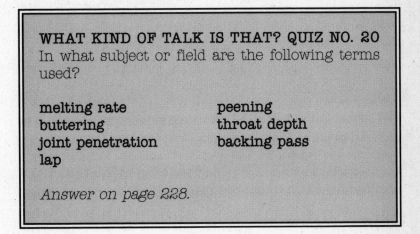

WHAT KIND OF TALK IS THAT? QUIZ NO. 20
In what subject or field are the following terms
used?

melting rate   peening
buttering   throat depth
joint penetration   backing pass
lap

Answer on page 228.

Blameless Name-Calling

Contrary to the old singsong children's verse, names can hurt almost as much as sticks and stones. At the very least, they can bother people quite a bit, and even more so when the targets don't know exactly what the names they are being called mean.

The following epithets are not at all foul, yet have a certain satisfying ring to them. They sound far worse than they mean, and you'll be a better person for sticking (and stoning) with them rather than with those tiresome four-letter words.

■   ■   ■

adulterator   one who adds to or corrupts something else
ambivert   one whose personality is a mix of introvert and extrovert
bestiarian   an animal lover
cockalorum   a conceited or self-important little man
cockshy   a butt of ridicule
cunctator   a procrastinator
deviationist   one who strays from an organization's beliefs

eructator   a belcher
homeopath   a practitioner of medicine favoring symptom-related dosages as a remedy
hypnobate   a sleepwalker
lucubrator   one who studies long into the night
masticator   a chewer
neophiliac   one loving anything new or novel
nympholept   one longing for an unattainable ideal
pedagogue   a teacher
philatelist   a stamp collector
preterist   one who lives in the past
privies in blood   blood relatives having certain rights or interest in the same estate
spermophobe   a fearer of germs
ultracrepidarian   a presumptuous overachiever
usufructuary   a user or enjoyer of another's property

WHAT KIND OF TALK IS THAT? QUIZ NO. 21
In what subject or field are the following terms used?

barn-door wipe	tongue
belly board	banana plug
china girl	diaphragm presetting
cradle head	hooking
dry box	creepie-peepie
swinger	abrasion marks
limpet mount	twang box

Answer on page 228.

In the early eighteenth century, ladies liked their hair in curls high off the forehead. To do this they wore a commode, or sometimes a wig with many dildos.

Fashion Warp: A History of Titivation

The terminology of historical clothing (or costume), cloth production, fabrics, and sewing can have some unkempt associative meanings. It can be a garb-le that's, well, a bad wrap. It's like a poor tailor who fails to acquire fabric of the right color. Start out with some white designs and you may end up with some blue material.

The names of old garments, in particular, can be unexpectedly exciting.

This is perhaps best illustrated by the following freshman paper, not at all out of whole cloth, on the history of clothing. It was composed by a first-year male student (who shall remain nameless) at the famed Costume and Fashion Institute.

The paper, though exhaustive in its use of garment and related terminology, was criticized for having no organizational plan, sloppy syntax, and poor transitions as well as non sequiturs. It did not receive a passing grade. The student is no longer at the institute.

THE HISTORY OF CLOTHING

From a woman's French beaver to a man's stiff and uncomfortable dickey, clothing has a varied and fascinating history. Its terminology can be tricky, as shown when the English poet Robert Browning wrote in the nineteenth century about the nun's twat. Apart from ordinary human beings, fashion affects animals, too. The ins and outs of dog fashion, for example, are more interesting and complicated than you may realize.

Cave people wore simple pelts, maybe three hides or four skins. Men and women have worn all variety of smocks, coats, leggings, kerchiefs, and hats over the centuries.

The ancient Egyptians liked to show off their flashy pectorals. Across the Mediterranean, the thoughtful Greek husband would sometimes greet his buxom wife with a bosom band. In ancient Rome, the boys could be fussy about the feminalia, and they loved to flaunt their paenula or toga virilis and see a female in cestus.

Centuries later, in Chaucer's day, a man always had an eye for a woman's suckeny, and the dapper gent was wont to waggle his smart and beaklike bycocket or maybe proffer a pearly choker to his wife. It could also be a brooch of taste. Later, collars were popular and many were into the ruff trade.

In the eighteenth century, strangely, men wore the chapeau bras, which could also be carried under the arm. A man was always proud of his hose. For a woman's head, a gentleman of the nineteenth century could give her either a kiss-me-quick or a crisp poke. A woman often wore a light garment to be seductive but a man could usually see through it. While ladies wore robes and frocks, gentlemen wore various jackets. In the sixteenth century a wife rarely saw her husband's jerkin off. In the nineteenth century a man who worried about his legs wore his antigropelos, while males with a little daring and flair slipped into French bottoms. Years later English male undergraduates had a thing for Oxford bags.

Given the filth of the olden times, a married or unmarried woman needed an all-purpose coverslut. When she was cold, she kept not one but both of her hands in her muff, though some thick belly wool would also help to keep her warm.

Colors, of course, have always been the web and woof of fashion. One person might prefer the French nude, another the Hooker's green. Shades can be subtle. A wife might favor a garment in the beige while her husband prefers her in the buff. Today's sportswear designers are fiercely competitive about colors and their season's "lines." For example, designer X may well be totally unscrupulous about getting a peek at designer Y's latest tan line.

Types of cloth have also varied over the centuries. A thick penistone was serviceable from the sixteenth to the nineteenth centuries, and in the seventeenth century a man would have been accustomed to the average woman's coarse and cheap marrymuffe. Whatever it was to be made, a seamstress needed a good drilling, a lasting frocking. If you were into lace, you paid freely for some Spanish blonde. For full-length dress, your fifteenth-century lady valued a gown woven out of richly colored puke. Puke is no longer in fashion, of course.

Today's thriving textile industry relies on advanced machines and special methods, from using a swingle to beat your flax to using a spanker (or clapper) to pound your woolens. No textile factory is complete without dickeys, a feeler, a sliver lapper, a balling head, and a licker-in, but slop padding, beating up, ball sizing, and wetting out can also be important processes, along with the liquor ratio.

From splits to a delicate friquette, cloth must be vigilantly watched and treated at all stages. A sectionally active worker has to watch her calender. Puckering, necking, furring, bursting strength, chafe marks, and piles are always considerations. Countless things must be attended to. After removal of stress, one has to hope for creep recovery, and when it comes to warp ends there must be an entering plan. Certain substances are particularly important. There is cutch, there is cunilate, and handling rayon can leave you with extruded latex. Whatever the manufacturing process, today's fabrics are wonderful and varied—from Japanese fukiye to East African shiti to Frenchback.

While the nineteenth-century American valued beaver fustian, somebody today might prefer to slip into Georgette or get some black coosong. In the 1930s, both males and females enjoyed the freedom of bi-swings. Nor let us forget the "leather" crowd or strokable pelts, from a coney lappet to a wavy breit schwantz, as opposed to your undressed kid.

Some mention should be made of clothing in more exotic climes. There is always the simple lap-lap when you want to get it on in a hurry, and loinclothed people of India have their Palambangs. And African craftspeople are always busy making nicely loose bou-bous. In colder climes, Eskimo women didn't want their coats to blow upward and kept them down with heavy dickey beads. Uniforms are also important in the history of clothing. Active privates have, for example, their undress blues and may also look for cheap bargains at mufti dives. As for pages who want to get ahead, they had better take a shine to their teat-studs.

In the average home, sewing, knitting, or embroidery can be useful skills—usually those of the woman of the house. A pioneer woman had her loud belcher. Today's sewers and menders have to know all about bar tacks, prick stitches, and darned patterns. If they want to embroider things, there is oriental couching, fagoting (for hourglass shapes), or good Norwegian hardanger, or one could always go to a bargello.

Hairdos, like clothing styles, seem to come and go, especially those of women. In the early eighteenth century ladies liked their hair in curls high off the forehead. To do this they wore a commode, or sometimes a wig with many dildos. Later in that century, ladies' husbands seemed to prefer banging chignons and got used to seeing their women's bulky rump furbelows. At some point, men asked women to please take off those Phrygian caps. When a

Swiss lady desired a colorful headdress, her husband often gave her a schlappe. As for men, a male always had his sporty cockup or snug hure and couldn't wait to get it on.

Stiffening was important beneath garments even in the seventeenth century, and for this a pair of bodies was useful. As women's clothes became increasingly uncomfortable, a revolution was needed, and many women were asking for it. Some were dying for it.

At certain times all ladies were incredibly modest. For example, from the sixteenth to the early eighteenth century women wore loo masks. But by the 1960s many girls had hot pants.

Today the fashion industry is probably more competitive than it's ever been. There have even been some obsessed rival designers who have broken into women's-store vitrines eager for a peek. In the end, as with other things, good taste is the thing. Some fashions seem almost criminal, not to mention accessories. For instance, nowadays, amazingly, even men adorn their lobes. But a male should never give a female a single small earring when she'd rather have a nice dangling pair.

In conclusion, fashions and clothing will always change, but every person has a right to his or her own toilet.

GLOSSARY

antigropelos   waterproof leggings

balling head   in worsted yarn manufacture, a device onto which fibers from a roller are wound

ball sizing   stiffening of warp yarn that is in rope or ball form

banging chignon   a woman's hairstyle of the 1770s, with a wide, flat loop of hair hanging down to the nape, often tied with a ribbon

bargello   a zigzag design used in needlepoint

bar tack   use of a single matching thread

beating up   forcing the weft into the cloth

beaver fustian   a heavy American material of the nineteenth century

belcher   a large blue spotted neckerchief

belly wool   wool from a sheep's belly, forelegs, or hind legs

bi-swing   an airy 1930s single-breasted sport jacket or suit having a rear set-in belt and deep pleats all the way up to the shoulder

bosom band   a fabric or leather band worn tied or pinned to the body by women of ancient Greece

bou-bou   a long, loose-fitting African garment for both sexes

breit schwantz   the fur or skin of a very young Karakul lamb, having a wavy appearance

buff   a light yellow color

bursting strength   a material's ability to withstand rupture by pressure

by-cocket   a fifteenth-century man's high-crowned hat with a beaklike point in front and a wide brim turned up in back

calender   a machine with cylinders for smoothing or glazing cloth

cestus   a belt worn by women in ancient Greece

chafe marks   the chafed appearance of silk, rayons, and other fabrics that develop loosened fibers when wet

o

three-cornered,
the arm

r

ld curls high off

ighteenth centu-

d bustle stuffed

clothes

orm

lrus tooth sewn

enth and eigh-

e

according to a

hreads are tied

bins in a shut-

acking is of a

like beaver or

s flared at the

French nude the color a...
friquette a fine machine...
frocking cloth suitable fo...
fukiye a type of eighteen...
furring fur lining or trim...
Georgette a strong, dull...
hardanger a type of Nor...
Hooker's green a shade...
hot pants very brief and...
hure a tight-fitting cap...
jerkin a sleeveless, hip—...
kiss-me-quick a small b...
lap-lap a South Pacific ...
lappet a loose-hanging ...
licker-in a roller on a c...
line a certain general cla...
liquor ratio in textiles,...
  (dye) used and that of...
loo mask a half-mask w...
  eighteenth centuries to...
marrymuffe a seventeen...
  or a garment made of...
muff a tubelike, often fu...
mufti civilian clothes
necking a sudden reduc...
  filaments
oriental couching a ty...
Oxford bags cuffed wid...
  dergraduates
paenula a sleeveless Ro...
pair of bodies a sevent...
  with stiff whalebone,...
Palambang a plain-wea...
  borders, used in India

chapeau bras   an eighteenth-century man's three-cornered, crescent-shaped hat that could be carried under the arm

choker   a collar of pearls or a fabric neckband

cockup   a hat with the brim turned up

commode   a silk-covered wire frame used to hold curls high off the forehead by women of the seventeenth and eighteenth centuries (also called a palisade)

coney   rabbit fur

coosong   a black-dyed plain-weave cotton cloth

cork rump   an eighteenth-century crescent-shaped bustle stuffed with cork

coverslut   an outer apron once worn over untidy clothes

creep recovery   a fabric's gradual returning to form

cunilate   a powerful mildew inhibitor

cutch   a resinous astringent and tanning extract

dickey   a man's detachable shirtfront

dickey bead   a pear-shaped piece of ivory or walrus tooth sewn near the bottoms of Eskimos' coats

dildos   sausage-shaped wig curls of the seventeenth and eighteenth centuries

drilling   a double cotton fabric with a twill weave

entering plan   a drawing-in draft of warp ends according to a particular plan

extruded latex   latex coagulated as viscose rayon

fagoting   a type of embroidery in which exposed threads are tied into groups having an hourglass shape

feeler   a loom device to replace nearby empty bobbins in a shuttle

feminalia   Roman close-fitting breeches

Frenchback   worsted fabric, whose corded twill backing is of a different weave than that of the face of the cloth

French beaver   European rabbit fur made to look like beaver or nutria

French bottoms   nineteenth-century men's trousers flared at the hems

French nude   the color alesan, a light brown

friquette   a fine machine-made lace

frocking   cloth suitable for a frock (dress)

fukiye   a type of eighteenth-century Japanese print

furring   fur lining or trimming

Georgette   a strong, dull-surfaced crepe fabric

hardanger   a type of Norwegian geometric embroidery

Hooker's green   a shade of green yellower than spearmint

hot pants   very brief and tight women's shorts

hure   a tight-fitting cap

jerkin   a sleeveless, hip-length, close-fitting man's jacket

kiss-me-quick   a small bonnet of the nineteenth century

lap-lap   a South Pacific loincloth

lappet   a loose-hanging fold or flap

licker-in   a roller on a carding machine (also called taker-in)

line   a certain general class of available commercial clothing

liquor ratio   in textiles, the ratio between the weight of a liquor (dye) used and that of the fibrous material

loo mask   a half-mask worn by women of the sixteenth through eighteenth centuries to cover the upper face

marrymuffe   a seventeenth-century coarse material for clothing, or a garment made of it

muff   a tubelike, often fur-covered warmer for a woman's hands

mufti   civilian clothes

necking   a sudden reduction in diameter when stretching undrawn filaments

oriental couching   a type of couched stitch; romanian stitch

Oxford bags   cuffed wide pants worn in the 1920s by Oxford undergraduates

paenula   a sleeveless Roman cloak, usually with a hood

pair of bodies   a seventeenth-century corset, often padded, made with stiff whalebone, wood, or steel

Palambang   a plain-weave cotton fabric having fancy decorative borders, used in India for loincloths and scarves

pectoral   an ancient Egyptian ornament with chain worn by important personages

penistone   a coarse woolen cloth used from the sixteenth to the nineteenth century

Phrygian cap   a limply conical but close-fitting cap

pile   a furry fabric surface

poke bonnet   a woman's bonnet with a projecting front brim

prick stitch   a short backstitch used on bulky fabrics

puckering   a crimped or folded effect

puke   a fifteenth-century high-quality fabric used for gowns

ruff   a starched and ornamentally pleated wheellike collar

rump furbelow   an eighteenth-century bustle in the form of a stuffed pad

schlappe   a picturesque Swiss headdress like a bonnet with side wings

shiti   an East African printed cotton dress fabric, generally with small floral designs in dark colors

sliver lapper   a textile machine that forms cotton slivers

slop padding   a type of resist textile printing

Spanish blonde   Spanish or French lace of a heavy pattern on a fine net ground

spanker   a block used to pound woolens flat (also called clapper)

splits   cloth having more than two selvage edges

suckeny   a smock

swingle   a two-foot wooden knifelike instrument used to beat flax

teat-stud   a metal button used primarily on jackets worn by pages

titivation   making smart or sprucing up

toga virilis   the Roman white toga of manhood

toilet   a person's particular dress or costume

twat   Browning's erroneous word (in *Pippa Passes*) for a nun's garment

undress blues   the military nondress uniform

undressed kid   kid leather finished with a nap surface
vitrine   a glass showcase
warp end   the end of a lengthwise thread
wetting out   an alkali boil or treatment with sulfonated oil to
  make cotton yarn more readily absorb water

WHAT KIND OF TALK IS THAT? QUIZ NO. 22
In what subject or field are the following terms
used?

foul matter	center spread
flush right	put to bed
bastard type	body type
jump head	recto
insert	

Answer on page 228.

■   ■   ■   ■   ■   ■   ■   ■   ■

GRAND EIGHT-WEEK TOUR OF EUROPE!

Unforgettable excursions to little-known communities of the Old World (tour is only for the Continent). Just the places to satisfy your wanderlust! You will visit:

Ballstad and Hell in Norway
Humppila in Finland
Hoor in Sweden
Kisserup and Balling in Denmark
Asselfingen, Assmannshausen, Buttenhausen, Kisslegg, Suckow, Humptrup, Humpl, Rumpen, Kockweg, Schwollen, Pissdorf, Nudersdorf, Bieswang, Cunsdorf, and Titisee in Germany
Kock, Panki, and Hel in Poland
Wangs, Grabs, and Cunter in Switzerland
Bangs in Austria
Horni Stubna in Czechoslovakia
Cuntis, Orgaz, Cuns, Sexmiro, Bra, Bozoo, Titaguas, Titulcia, Peniscola, Vulveralla, Hornes, Horno, Pusa, Rambla de los Nudos, and El Buste in Spain
Harderwijk, Asschat, De Cocksdorp, Donge, Dijk, Fokshol, Fochteloo, Gassel, Kokkengen, Koks, Loo, Raamsdonk, and Assen in the Netherlands
Mammola, Bra, Testico, and Monte Nudo in Italy
Pussemange, Asse, and Bra in Belgium

Puke in Albania
Turda in Romania
Bitche, Condom, Arsy, Conty, Pussay, Bust, Sexcles,
  and Loos-en-Gohelle in France
Kuntuk, Pap, Khakass Autonomous Oblast, Kok-
  bel, the Gory Putana Mountains, Dorka, Kuntchi,
  Koktunlik, Slutsk, Bum, and Vagino in the for-
  mer Soviet Union
Mammari in Cyprus
Budafok in Hungary
Bigadic in Turkey
Licko Lesce in former Yugoslavia
Klitoria in Greece
Frigg gas field in the North Atlantic

FOR DETAILS AND BOOKINGS, CONTACT GLOBE-TROTS TRAVEL
AGENCY

■   ■   ■   ■   ■   ■   ■   ■   ■

"Never mind the pasties and other tit-bits, I rather fancy your scrumptious bath buns."

Censorable British

The English have always insisted that they originated our language, and of course they named it after themselves. To them, American English is at best an aberration from the genuine article (an Englishman would never say "the real McCoy"). As Oscar Wilde commented, "We have really everything in common with America nowadays, except, of course, language."

To us Americans, though, the Brits have got some curious ways of saying things. They can also get very bloody-minded (unappreciative) when Yanks try to correct them. This is especially true when it is American FCC censors who are doing the correcting.

As the irate letter that follows makes clear, over a period of a year or so numerous lines from scripts for the popular imported radio program "Britannia Radio Theatre" were either bleeped out or altered by American radio censors for being "filthy and obscene." This letter of protest was sent to our State Department by angry British radio executives and writers, who are still awaiting an explanation. Why, in God's and the Queen's name, they ask, were these innocuous lines censored?

The lines in question also appear below. We reprint them here solely in the interests of mutual understanding and the hope that this issue may soon be resolved.

■ ■ ■

Department of State
"The Colonies"
Washington, District of Columbia

Dear Mr. Secretary,

As conjoined representatives of the British Britcasting Corporation, Piccadilly Wireless Playhouse, and Heaviside Layer Productions, we should like to strongly protest at the gratuitous censorship by your sundry state network authorities of numerous lines of dialogue in "Britannia Radio Theatre" programmes aired in your secessional country over the past year.

We supply herewith, below, the particular lines in question—each of which was wantonly and needlessly excised from a particular British wireless play, evidently out of some misguided Stateside notion that the lines were improper or sexually suggestive. Rest assured, they are nothing of the sort. All are perfectly sound *English* idioms, at least to those of us who dwell on this side of the Atlantic.

What conceivable untoward meanings can benighted American radio censors find, witlessly, in these perfectly apt and most innocuous conversational phrasings penned by respected, prize-winning British writers?

Jus et norma loquendi!

In testament whereof, we append here, with the unjustly censored lines, a glossary, noblesse oblige, for the edification of proscriptive Americans, new to our venerable language

and purblinded, as ever, by their bemusing Puritanical tradi-
tions.

We, the undersigned, demand an explanation.

Yours truly,
The British Radio Artists Group

I say, would you drive me to the nearest licensed house? *(Jill and Jack)*

Never mind the pasties and other tit-bits, I rather fancy your scrumptious bath buns. *(The Unholy Barrister)*

Rest assured, my husband dear, I shan't be found nosing around at any balls with such a clever dick. *(Little Bea and Big Ben)*

The chief inspector and I feel the firmness of your impressive chimney breast no longer needs looking into, Lady Wickingham. But your loose-box and bathroom tringle are another matter entirely. *(House of Trepidation)*

Regarding your drop-head, madam—this old layshaft seems a bit clapped out, and we'd better have a closer look at your big-end. *(A Yank in Yeovil)*

Married or not, Alec, every red-blooded man needs a good daily, and I've got Sweet Fanny Adams. Well, time to show a leg! *(I Say!)*

Celia, you hardly found Lord Cogham's dickey uncomfortable last week at the noisy rally with all those brazen hooters. *(An Extra Scone)*

Feeling a bit dicky, Lord Crowden? *(An Odd Yob)*

Tie me up in the Tower of London, and I still wouldn't eat these disgusting faggots or bangers. Nor does brawn enchant me. *(Little Bea and Big Ben)*

It's decidedly a tickler for the French, but you had bloody well bet I'm vexed by such a cock-up. *(Knickers and Snickers)*

Believe me, Geoffrey, tidying up after the firm's bean-feast was a real stinker last year. *(The Tradesman's Entrance)*

When she was called to the bar, Lady Wells felt it incumbent on her to give tongue to all manner of cock. *(A Visit to the Ironmonger)*

I've long had a rod in pickle for you, faithless wench, and it's time I gave it to you hot. *(The Ivied Tower)*

All young Steven seems to care about is flogging his precious whizzbang, and whenever he's about he gives me the hump. *(The Mystery of the Duvet)*

I know you've been stepping out with a fruiterer on Mincing Lane. *(The Gay Blade of Whitechapel)*

My good man, it's especially for the Queen's proctor, and the lady's finger is essential. *(The Unholy Barrister)*

Blimey, I offers her a kind hand with her sizable and heavy jugs—in the reign of Queen Dick, she says! *(An Extra Scone)*

I'm tired of lying doggo for days on end and putting up with the grunting of your cack-handed physical jerks when you're not paying your whack! *(A Busker Too Many)*

It was their first night, and that gazumping Old Horney made those unlicked, hard-working girls make do with a strip-wash. *(On Stage, Please!)*

Joe Wilcox is the shire's legendary lengthman, always hard at it, but the locals are quite put out by these dangerous unstable verges and beguiling centre strips. *(Ponces at Large)*

She got quite pissed on plonk last night, and one's approach had jolly well be deep-laid before he ventures to knock her up this morning. *(House of Trepidation)*

I say, would you tidy up that slut's wool along the skirting? Tomorrow I must engage a chippie who can show me a thing or two about a damp course and deals—some good planking. *(Your Naughty Waspie)*

Call me a bit of a crock, if you will, but I'm happy to say I'm under the doctor at this very moment. *(I Say!)*

Sis says she's easy, so I takes her out in the car and tells her she better well do it, neck or nothing. *(Knickers and Snickers)*

Deirdre was only my sleeping partner, and needed some licking into shape. *(An Extra Scone)*

Now, there's a lady who's really knackered and easy to score off! *(Voices from the Boot)*

At the moment Gwyneth is in the outhouse—I'd be quite glad to see the back of her. *(Watch Over the Thames)*

Would you fancy holding my whinger, old cock, before I do my nut? *(Jewel of the Desert)*

It was admittedly a tease, but when she so casually pinched that teat, I tore a strip off her. *(All's Well That Doesn't End)*

I confronted him right in the stalls, where I lost no time in wiping off a score. *(The Rowhouse Mystery)*

I believe My Lord encountered Black Rod—a queer stick, they say. *(An Odd Yob)*

She wasn't exactly wet about letting him blithely sport his oak. *(House of Trepidation)*

Vanessa, if you're not prospering as a shop-walker or with shilling shockers, what about a wages-snatch? *(The Tradesman's Entrance)*

If we were in arsy-versy positions—I don't mean to cheek you—I wouldn't want to be done down or blown. *(First Train to Blackpool)*

When the clippie came to me to unbelt before that lay-by—what a box-up!—I reached into my trousers pocket. Not a sausage! *(I Say!)*

Blimey if I shouldn't like to bone her casket and hump it away and see her far enough. *(A Busker Too Many)*

I intend no jiggery-pokery or to come it rather strong, sir, but indeed she makes a lovely bedder. *(Pardon Me Mum)*

It's about bargains with my daughter concern and Malaysian godown, and there's this slight problem with stuffing and stripping. *(City Business)*

Would you have some rubbers? I'm afraid I'm a compulsive masticator and am always using them up. *(An Extra Scone)*

Mr. Smith: What do you see as your chief needs here, Mrs. Cuthbert?

Mrs. Cuthbert: As many imaginative and resourceful boffins as I can get. *(The Mystery of the Duvet)*

I want an attractive gent, not a grotty little turkey cock. *(Voices from the Boot)*

Let me put it this way: You might do well to knock yourself up a bit. *(A Yank in Yeovil)*

She's rather sluttish and keen on foretime, but he's a stroppy thruster, always eager to give a new secretary a good towelling. *(Knickers and Snickers)*

What would you ask in the West Country for your scrumpy firkin? *(Miranda's Secret)*

A young girl, very big on pictures of the royals, asked if I wanted to see her Regina. *(The Unholy Barrister)*

Julia is quite switched on and sees nothing wrong with brothel-creepers. *(The Empire of Young Julia)*

I'm for a bit of spotted dick! *(Incident on Regent Street)*

The little woman can handle my thermic lance, but of course she's not very adept with blowcocks. *(A Visit to the Ironmonger)*

Bob and me, we hadn't much more than a couple of stale old swedes in the house, so we drove over to the Broads to find a decent chippy open for business. *(Voices from the Boot)*

Margaret Pelter, who's just been taken on as a mistress by Head-master Collins, has the most darling, strokable rumpy. *(Country Ways)*

Danny's a criminal type and cares only about a good spanker and a trusty funk hole. *(The Gay Blade of Whitechapel)*

Group Captain Worthington has many a tale about problems with air screws. *(Squadron in Jeopardy)*

My squiffers and hand organ have hair cracks and are delicate, love, so please do not fondle. *(Little Bea and Big Ben)*

At the sight of Mrs. Elliot's hotted up figgy duff, Worthington felt himself turning queer. *(Only at a Pinch!)*

Reluctantly, we went up together to this WPC. The stuckup little madam was seated on a tip-up seat, looking as though we were expected to compliment her on her nice pair of Darbies. *(The Road to Bournemouth)*

Julia, who herself was a top-hole understrapper in the sweet trade, had gotten her monkey up, and by now she was getting on Leonard's wick. *(I Say!)*

Ronnie desperately wanted to take her by the force, but they were still nose to tail well before the double bend. *(The Final Call)*

Michael, who denied he'd been feeling this brain fag, suddenly came over queer the night he did a midnight flit. *(Voices from the Boot)*

Juggins or not—I know about her monstrous bloomers and boobs—I shall nonetheless be at the back of this Deborah Withers. *(London Interlude)*

Look slippy! We simply can't do these things on top of each other. *(The Problem of Mrs. Cates)*

Catherine was married, had a charming pigeon pair, and was hot to go to a knees up. *(Ticket to Portobello Road)*

The workers were eating their jocks, and one of the blokes had some grouty dick going gash. *(The Unholy Barrister)*

GLOSSARY

air screw   an aircraft propeller

arsy-versy   in reverse, backwards, or vice versa

at the back of   behind or in support of

banger   a sausage

bar   the profession of barrister

bath bun   a type of sweet bun with spices and dried fruit; also, a crone

bean-feast   a company picnic or any merry occasion

bedder   an annual plant that can be grown in a garden bed; also, a room cleaner at Cambridge University

big-end a car's rod (control) bearing
bloomer a blunder in speech
blowcock a tap on a boiler
blown (to be blown) to be found out
boffin a scientific expert
bone to swipe or make off with
boob a blunder in speech
box-up a mix-up
brain fag mental exhaustion
brawn headcheese
brazen hooter a brass car horn
Broads the Norfolk Broads, a low-lying area, with waterways
brothel-creepers crepe-soled suede shoes
cack-handed clumsy (left-handed)
casket a small box for valuables
centre strip a road's median divider or "central reserve"
cheek to be impudent or rude to
chimney breast a projecting chimney wall
chippie a carpenter
chippy a fish-and-chips shop
clapped out worn out or dilapidated
clever dick a smug and conceited know-it-all
clippie a bus conductress
cock nonsense
cockshy a target in a throwing game
cock-up a mess or muddle
come it rather strong to lay it on thick
come over queer to become dizzy
crock a broken-down person
daily a cleaning woman
damp course an insulating layer
Darbies handcuffs
daughter concern a subsidiary
deal a plank or piece of lumber
deep-laid well thought out or planned

dickey   (or dickey box) a rumble seat in a carriage

dicky   shaky or queasy

do a midnight flit   to move surreptitiously or at night, as to avoid paying one's rent or debts

do (one) down   to do someone dirt or humiliate her or him

do one's nut   to work like mad; to blow one's top

double bend   an S curve in the road

drop-head   a convertible (car)

easy   (I'm easy) it's all the same to me

exhibitioner   a student awarded an exhibition

faggot   a ball of chopped meat and herbs

figgy duff   a steamed pudding with raisins or currants

firkin   a barrel containing nine imperial gallons

first night   opening night at the theater

flog   to sell

fondle   to touch (an article or goods in a store)

force   (Northern England) a waterfall

foretime   old times or the past

fruiterer   a fruit seller

funk hole   a hideout

gash   extra or spare

gazump   to jack up the price or to swindle

Gentleman Usher of the Black Rod   an officer of the Order of the Garter

get one's monkey up   to become angry

get on one's wick   to get one's goat

give it to (one) hot   to punish or thrash

give (one) the hump   to depress or get another's spirits down

give tongue to   to talk or cry

go-down   a warehouse of the Far East

grotty   seedy or dirty

grouty dick   a Black Country (smoky and grimy districts in Staffordshire and the West Midlands) pudding, made with suet and raisins

hair crack   a hairline crack

hand organ   a barrel organ (or street piano)
hard at it   working hard
have a rod in pickle for   to be longing to punish
hooter   a car horn
hot up   to warm up or heat again
hump   to carry or lug
in the reign of Queen Dick   never
jiggery-pokery   deceitful behavior or business; trickery
jock   (Lancashire dialect) a snack eaten during a work break
jug   a pitcher
juggins   a simpleton
knackered   tired out or tuckered out
knees up   a lively party with dancing
knock oneself up   to knock oneself out with exertion
knock (one) up   to wake someone
lady's finger   okra (used in Indian cooking)
lay-by   a rest stop along a highway
layshaft   a car transmission's countershaft
lengthman   a road maintenance man
licensed house   a pub or saloon
lick into shape   to make satisfactory
lie doggo   to be in hiding or out of sight
look slippy   to hurry up
loose-box   a horse stall
loose chippings   gravel
madam   a conceited young woman
masticator   a chewer
Mincing Lane   the tea business (and a London street)
mistress   one of the teaching staff at a girls' school
neck or nothing   at any cost or at whatever the risk
nose to tail   bumper to bumper
not a sausage   nothing; not a damned thing
old cock   (familiarly or fondly) old man
Old Horny   the Devil
on top of each other   all at once

outhouse   an outbuilding or incidental building
pasties   pies filled with meat and potatoes
pay one's whack   to chip in
physical jerks   physical exercises or calisthenics
pigeon pair   boy and girl twins, or a boy and girl who are a family's only two children
pinch   to steal
pissed   drunk
plonk   table or house wine
Queen's proctor   an official who can intervene in divorce cases
queer stick   an odd or strange person
Regina   official title of the reigning queen
rubber   an eraser
rumpy   a Manx cat
score off   to get the better of
scrumpy   a rough cider of the West Country
see (one) far enough   to see one in hell
see the back of   to see the last of
shilling shocker   a dime novel or "penny dreadful"
shop-walker   a floorwalker
show a leg   to get up in the morning; rise and shine
sitting bodkin   being squeezed sitting between two other people
skirting   a baseboard
sleeping partner   a silent partner in business
slut's wool   dust balls
sluttish   idle; untidy
spanker   a fast horse
sport (one's) oak   to tell everybody to stay out; hang out the Do Not Disturb sign
spotted dick   (also spotted dog) a suet pudding with raisins or currants
squiffer   a concertina
stalls   the orchestra in a theater
stinker   a difficult problem or task
strip-wash   a sponge bath

stroppy bad-tempered or aggressive
stuffing and stripping in marine transport, the packing and un-
  packing of containers
swede a yellow turnip
Sweet Fanny Adams absolutely nothing
sweet trade the candy or confectionary business
switched-on trendy or up-to-date
take one's dick to take an oath
tear a strip off (someone) to bawl out
tease a tricky job
teat the rubber bulb of a medicine dropper
thermic lance a blowtorch
thruster a ruthlessly ambitious person
tickler a tricky problem or delicate situation
tip-up seat a folding seat
tit-bits tidbits
top-hole first-rate
towelling a thrashing
tringle a curtain rod
turkey cock a conceited person
turn queer to become nauseated or ill
unbelt to shell out (money)
understrapper a subordinate or underling
under the doctor under the doctor's care
unlicked immature or having poor manners
unstable verge a "soft shoulder" on a road
wages snatch a payroll holdup
wet dumb or stupid
whinger a dirk (long dagger)
whitebait edible sprats or young fish
whizzbang a firework
wipe off a score to settle a score
WPC Woman Police Constable, or policewoman

WHAT KIND OF TALK IS THAT? QUIZ NO. 23
In what subject or field are the following terms used?

honey sump   laying worker
slumgum   balling a queen

Answer on page 228.

"Would you like to sniff
my prickmadam?"

Earthy and
Seedy Talk

Just as plants must be handled with care and delicacy, so must their proper names. Even a professional horticulturist, who may nurture or rearrange nature beautifully—spill seed in just the right places, oversee an artistic bower movement, give a copse a "feel"—had better know his furzes from his spurges or his grass will be ass parsley. It is very hard for the surprisingly pungent language of plant life, the semantic succulence of flora, to be, well, soft-petaled.

Plants all have their Latin genus-species names. But uttering the more popular and regional names—and their less familiar variant names—could easily get any scientific botanist or weekend gardener into a whole plot of trouble.

This year's Peasecod Flower Show was written up by volunteer novice reporter Gladys Willard for *The Peasecod Times.* Here, to convey in one piece all the semantic excitement of plant life, is Gladys's article.

FROM COLDFRAMES TO HOTBEDS!

Talk about a growth industry!

Our justly famed annual Peasecod Flower Show was held this weekend on the lovely grounds of the old Weems estate, with its spacious, crystalline conservatory. It drew people from states far and wide and, as always, our local pride was in full blossom! All the experts in heaving, pricking out, pinching back, and hardening off were present. Could I take a "leaf" from their book? You bet your wild ash!

One thing I didn't count on was my old allergies acting up. Your brave reporter sneezed her way through the exhibition! We also had a mysterious plant thief on the loose! Both mysteries were solved before I left, and both had the same culprit!

The Peasecod show is always the perfect place to peddle your aster, indulge your hortulan mongering, or let go with your nymphaeum mania! It was also a horticultural education for this reporter, who has more of a hitchhiker's thumb than a green thumb! Hitherto I owed all my knowledge of growing things to an old boyfriend, who introduced me to blowballs in the nearby meadow. Alas, I don't know from shittah, but with the handsome Peasecod show program and directory in hand, I "planted" myself wherever I could hobnob with the throngs of greenery lovers and listen in. I learned about everything from Peeping Toms to compact Korean boxes.

Lovely New Age music, not too loud, set a nice mood. And "Mr. Green Thumb" was to be seen strolling up and down the aisles everywhere. Mr. Green Thumb was (I think!) a genial young person in a green-tights costume with a tall head mask like a green thumb, complete with thumb nail, much like a Gumby or Cone Head. He was friendly to everyone. From a big green sack, he passed out free packages of plant food. Beneath his thumb head, I sniffed, he was wearing a sexy after-shave!

As your roving reporter, I did my best to note and identify at least some of the plants and to pick up fascinating conversational snatches. There was one sour note. Shortly after I arrived with pad and pencil in hand, it was announced on the PA system that an expensive bonsai had been reported missing and presumably stolen. Security guards had their eyes peeled. Who would do such a thing?

But I was in plant heaven! Everything seemed freshly watered, and I noticed two men at a big flower stand shaking the dew off their lilies. Even trees, or tree seedlings, and rare ones at that, were well represented. I saw some nice stinking cedars. There was also a Eurasian open-arse and a stinking ash. One exhibitor was comparing French cherry with oriental cherry while visitors near him admired a red titi, Philippine danglin, and a shortshat. But in no time at all I was sneezing my little nose off. Me, allergic to certain plants and covering a greenery show!

Most green-thumbers, of course, were more interested in smaller plants—all those herbs, ferns, nettles, vines, and vetches. Everybody was friendly, helpful, or both, like one young man with a sprinkler who was busy watering an older lady's bubbybush. She was soon desperate to find a common privet. At one stand two attractive young ladies were selling some brand of freeze-dried celebrity nightsoil called Star Droppings. What will they think of next!

Herbs were the topic of the day with one group of devotees I overheard.

"I've got some navelworts and nippleworts," I heard Ms. Ida Smith saying to her friend Sam Wycoff. "But I'm looking for a kidney vetch. How are your blue balls, Sam?"

"Hanging in there," Sam replied. "That's a lovely Victorian box you have there. You know, I just saw some beautiful lady pea here. For me, there's nothing like quick-in-the-hand. Would you like to sniff my prickmadam?"

Ida replied that she found prickmadam interesting as a kind of folk medicine. "But if I were going to plump for anything of mine this year, it would be my two queen-cups and floppers. And look at my nice-smelling origan, and my lovely hindberry!"

"Thank God this year there's no bastard horehound or gas

plant here," remarked one of Ida's friends, whose name I didn't catch.

"Do they have any naked lady here?" another gentleman inquired. He was also interested in either fringed pink or old-maid's pink and a Malayan gebang.

"I believe so," Ida's friend informed him. "Over by the witch hazel and naked broom rape. I've already got myself a wall pellitory and will probably take a wild leek and a roof houseleek after I find myself an Abyssinian banana, an Indian poke, and a black medic."

As Mr. Green Thumb strolled by, Ida's friend let Sam admire her creamcups and hoary puccoon. Sam thought they were quite nice but indicated that for a real succulent, there was nothing like his wife's French pusley. Another gentleman nearby remarked that what he really wanted to bring back home was some boy's-love, hairy fairybells, a Bristol fairy, a tall gay-feather, a bedding pansy, a flaming pinkster, and a few California fairy fans. At this point, I uncontrollably sneezed in his face and received quite a dirty look.

My friendly little group of herb-lovers was still chatting about queen's-delight, little-boy's breeches, dysentery weed, and varieties of *Clitoria* when I moved on. Near an Australian gentleman who was answering questions about the motherumbung, burrawang, bangalow, lillypilly, and bangalay, I encountered three out-of-state ladies excited about ferns, vines, vetches, and cacti. They were comparing purchases.

"I see you've got a most luxuriant bush vetch," said one.

"Yes. My husband always liked my cushcush yam and climbing maidenhair, so I thought I'd try a bush vetch. Do you know anything about hairy lip fern?"

"What a nice adder's tongue! I don't know from hairy lip fern, though my sister has a big farm and I could show you a Polaroid of her hairy vetch and finger fern. May I see your privet lippia?"

The others oohed and aahed at the picture of her sister's hairy vetch (not to be confused with a slender vetch, I'm told). They compared notes on creepers, both the five-fingered and the fairy varieties, and talked about a man met earlier looking for an afternoon lady and a female fluellen. The three women soon turned to the topic of prickly flora, from bullsuckers to feather balls and nipple cacti. An elegantly dressed gentleman nearby proudly displayed his big red prickly pear while he identified for me some tropical coonties and wonderful-smelling labiates. He was looking for a mother-of-thousands or at least a wild date.

I was out of tissues by now. My worst moment came when I sneezed on some woman's newly purchased cactus. She accused me of being a plant killer—and of much worse!

"Have you seen a good West Indian dildo anywhere?" the obese woman asked. But her companions were already drifting away. At one booth a woman who was an expert on grass answered questions for people with creeping bent or brown bent as well as some from a West Coast resident concerned about her lady hair grass, pusstail, and soft cheat. Other questions were about the genera *Pennisetum* and *Quamoclit.*

A tree auctioneer, meanwhile, had brought to his platform two exemplary black titis and, with its edible nutlike seed, a stout wankapin, a shadblow serviceberry, and an assacu, not to mention two dugdugs. Next to a demonstration of a force bed, one group discussed base horehounds. Nearby, I got my first good look at St.-Jacob's-dipper and St.-Anthony's-nut while two teenage girls, each with a small French furze, were listening to an old gardener talking about his sleepy Dick and failing pussytoes.

A larger group listened nearby to an agriculture professor's informative talk on seeds, drupes, and the like. Even Mr. Green Thumb paused to listen. I had another sneezing attack, and several people in the crowd shushed me. The lecturer had some asses'-eyes and some false wild oats, and he showed around some rapeseed and virgin dip. When he asked his audience a question about plant poisons, one listener threw up nux vomica at him. Quite correctly! The professor's lame attempt at humor—"Show me a lady's-delight and I'll show you a wild pansy"—fell a bit flat. Besides, many of his bored listeners seemed to want to go badly, a few of them going to the close-by Japanese privet and shiitake table, others to the *Lavatera*. Others milled around a tree exhibitor who was displaying two genipaps and a two-eye berry. A vendor all the way from Wales invited me to take a leek free.

For old-fashioned romantics, there was a choice between kiss-me-at-the-gate, love's-test, love-lies-bleeding, and love-in-a-mist.

The main attractions at the Peasecod show, of course, were flowers, shrubs, and certain special plants. From blue dicks to coral blows, from dangleberries to cover-shames, from French cockleburs to Hottentot cherries and Hottentot figs, from May blobs to all kinds of pissabeds, from Jacob's-rod to Johnny cocks, from smelling-stick to pukeweek, it was a banner day for greenery!

Some time before I left, there was a commotion as two guards detected the thief of the expensive bonsai. After finding the delicate plant inside his big green plant food sack, the guards led Mr. Green Thumb away. I never sneezed once in the next hour. Obviously it was Mr. Green Thumb's after-shave, not a plant, that I had been allergic to!

I never got to the seminar on uredinology, the movie about *Funkia,* the lecture on the mossy vaginula, or the one on extramatrical activity. I never got to see one woman's prize-winning feverbush or her husband's stiff bushpoppy. I avoided the stinking poke, stinking Roger, and stinkhorn! But on my way out I did see a lovely West Indian lady-of-the-night. A vender, who gave me a rush, tried to sell me a lady's bedstraw, and then to take off on his shoes and stocking. He also had a catjang. Instead, I took a darling pea, then a glory pea.

Next year, I want a chaste tree!

GLOSSARY

Abyssinian banana   the ensete, a banana tree
adder's tongue   a fern of the genus *Ophioglossum*

afternoon lady the four-o'clock, a common garden plant with fragrant yellow, red, and white flowers

assacu the sandbox tree, a tropical American tree with capsules that burst loudly

asses'-eyes the seeds of the cowhage

ass parsley fool's parsley, a poisonous European weed

bangalay an Australian tree with a hard and durable wood (also called bastard mahogany or woolly butt)

bangalow a lofty Australian feather-palm

base horehound the white dead nettle, a European prickly herb

bastard horehound an ill-smelling European herb (also called fetid horehound, stinking horehound, black horehound)

bedding pansy a European violet (also called horned violet or tufted pansy)

black medic an annual prostrate herb, a lawn weed

black titi a tree of the southern United States with glossy leaves and white flowers (also called titi or buckwheat tree)

blowball a fluffy seed ball, like the dandelion

blue ball the blue scabius, a European herb

blue dicks the wild hyacinth, a North American bulbous plant

bonsai a Japanese potted dwarf plant

boy's-love the southernwood, a shrubby European wormwood

Bristol fairy a herbaceous perennial flower that blooms through the summer

brown bent the dog bent, a common grass with narrow leaves

bubbybush the Carolina allspice

bullsucker any of various West Indian cacti

burrawang any Australian plant of the genus *Macrozamia*

bush vetch a European purple-flowered vetch

California fairy fan an annual herb with fan-shaped petals

catjang the pigeon pea

chaste tree the agnus castus, an ornamental shrub with blue and white flowers

climbing maidenhair a climbing fern

Clitoria a genus of herbs and woody vines

common privet the privet *Ligustrum vulgare*

coontie a woody plant of tropical America

coral blow the coral plant, a largely leafless Mexican shrub

cover-shame the savin, a largely prostrate Eurasian juniper having dark foliage and small berries

creamcup a California annual of the Papaveraceae family

creeping bent a common pasture or lawn grass (also called creeping bentgrass)

cushcush yam a herbaceous twining vine cultivated for its edible tubers

dangleberry a huckleberry having pink flowers and sweet blue fruit

danglin a Philippine tree whose coarse fiber is used in making rope

darling pea either of two Australian plants with racemose flowers

dildo a West Indian spiny cactus with pink flowers

dugdug the fertile form of the breadfruit tree

dysentery weed a biennial North American herb having prickly barbed fruit (also called dysentery root or Virginia stickseed)

extramatrical describing aerial parts of parasitic fungi that lie outside a substratum

fairy creeper the climbing fumitory, a vine with feathery leaves and flowers

false wild oats an aberrant form of cultivated oats (also called fatuoid)

feather ball a low tuberculate Mexican cactus with feathery white spines

female fluellen the germander speedwell, a European herb

feverbush the spicebush, an aromatic shrub with yellow flowers succeeded by bright red or yellow berries

finger fern the scale fern

five-fingered creeper the Virginia creeper, a common North American tendril-climbing vine with bluish-black berries

flaming pinkster the flame azalea

floppers any of several plants whose leaves yield new plants (also called air plant or life plant)

force bed a hotbed for forcing early plant growth

French cherry the Surinam cherry, a Brazilian tree from whose spicy red fruit jelly is made

French cocklebur the Caesar weed, a tropical shrub that yields a strong woody fiber

French furze the common furze

French pusley a tropical succulent herb with yellow, pink, red, white, or purple flowers

fringed pink any of several pinks, especially a Eurasian perennial herb

Funkia a small genus of the lily family

gas plant the fraxinella, a European perennial herb whose flowers give off a flammable vapor in hot weather

gayfeather a purple-flowered perennial herb

gebang a Malayan fan palm

genipap a tree, with edible fruit, of the West Indies and South America

glory pea a cleanthus having usually red flowers

hairy fairybells a hairy perennial herb with greenish flowers and red fruits

hairy lip fern the woolly lip fern, a small North American fern

hairy vetch the hairy tare, a European vetch cultivated as a cover and for forage

hardening-off gradually reducing water and temperature for plants grown indoors in order to toughen their tissues

heaving the thrusting of plants out of the ground caused by alternate freezing and thawing during the winter

hindberry the common red raspberry of Europe

hoary puccoon a North American perennial herb with hairy foliage

hortulan relating to a garden or gardening

Hottentot cherry a South African plant with handsome foliage

houseleek   a common European succulent with pink flowers, found on old walls and roofs

Indian poke   the hellebore (herb) *Viratrum viride*

Jacob's-rod   the asphodel, an herb

Japanese privet   either of two Asiatic evergreen ornamental shrubs used for hedges

Johnny cocks   the male orchis, a Eurasian orchid

kidney vetch   a perennial Eurasian herb with red or yellow flowers, once used as a remedy for kidney problems

kiss-me-at-the-gate   a fragrant Chinese honeysuckle grown ornamentally in the southern United States

Korean box   the hardiest box (shrub) of all

labiate   any plant of the mint family

lady hair grass   the quaking grass

lady-of-the-night   a West Indian shrub with fragrant yellowing white flowers

lady pea   the cowpea, a sprawling herb of the Old World tropics cultivated in the southern United States for forage

lady's-bedstraw   a common bedstraw with yellow flowers (also called yellow bedstraw or cleavers)

lady's-delight (or ladies'-delight)   a common European herb (also called heartsease, wild pansy, or johnny-jump-up)

Lavatera   a genus of shrubs, herbs, and trees of the mallow family

leek   an edible garden herb associated with Welsh patriotism

lillypilly   an Australian tree with hard, fine-grained wood

little-boy's breeches   the Dutchman's-breeches, a delicate spring-flowering herb

love-in-a-mist   a European garden plant; also, a tropical American passionflower

love-lies-bleeding   a cultivated plant of the genus *Amaranthus*

love's test   an everlasting (a plant that keeps its color and form when dried) of eastern North America

May blob   the marsh marigold, a swamp herb

mossy vaginula   part of a moss's archigonium

mother-of-thousands   the beefsteak saxifrage, or creeping-sailor

motherumbung   an Australian shrub with flowers in pairs or threes (also called motherumbah)

naked broom rape   a caucerroot of North America

naked lady   the meadow saffron

nap-at-noon   the star-of-Bethlehem, an Old World herb with greenish flowers

navelwort   a European succulent herb

nipple cactus   any cactus of the genus *Neomamillaria*

nipplewort   an annual herb with heads of yellow flowers

nux vomica   the poisonous seed of an Asian tree

nymphaeum   a classic building used for plants and flowers

old-maid's pink   the corn cockle, an annual herb

open-arse   the medlar, a Eurasian tree having fruit like crabapples

oriental cherry   the Japanese flowering cherry

origan   the wild marjoram, a Eurasian perennial herb

Peeping Tom   a yellow variety of narcissus

Pennisetum   a genus of Old World grasses

pinching back   the shortening of young shoots to enhance their growth or development

pissabed   any of numerous wild plants, such as the daisy or dandelion

pricking out (or pricking off)   the transplanting of tiny seedlings into flats

prickly pear   a cactus with flat joints and rounded or barrel shaped fruit

prickmadam   any of various stonecrops (an herb)

privet lippia   an aromatic shrub and troublesome invader Southwestern U.S. grassland

pukeweed   the Indian tobacco, an American wild lobelia

pussytoe (or pussy's toe)   a type of cat's-foot (ground ivy eastern and central North America

Quamoclit   a genus of twining vines, or a plant of this ger

queen-cups   a perennial herb of the Rocky Mountains

queen's-delight a perennial herb whose root is used medicinally

quick-in-the-hand the jewelweed, a glaucous annual herb with yellow to white flowers sometimes having brownish-red spots

rapeseed the seed of the rape, used for an oil

red titi the leatherwood *Cyrilla racemiflora*

rush a marsh plant

St.-Anthony's-nut an earthnut

St.-Jacob's-dipper the pitcher plant

shadblow serviceberry a shrubby tree grown for its white flowers and red-purple fruit

shiitake an edible large black or brown mushroom

shittah a tree, believed to be the acacia, mentioned in the Bible

shoes and stocking the bird's-foot trefoil, a European plant with pods used as fodder

shortshat the shortleaf pine

sleepy Dick the star of Bethlehem, an Old World herb with greenish flowers

slender vetch a European vetch with blue or purple flowers

smelling-stick the common North American sassafras

soft cheat a weedy grass of the Old World

stiff bushpoppy an evergreen shrub grown for its yellow flowers

stinkhorn a malodorous phallic-shaped fungus

stinking ash the box elder

stinking cedar the fetid yew, a Florida evergreen tree with malodorous leaves

stinking poke the skunk cabbage

stinking Roger any of various ill-smelling plants

tall gayfeather a herbaceous perennial with purple flowers

two-eye berry the partridgeberry, a trailing plant

uredinology a branch of mycology (fungi) dealing with rusts

Victorian box the native laurel, an Australian evergreen tree with shiny leaves and white flowers

virgin dip first-year resin from a tree tapped for turpentine

wall pellitory a European wall-growing herb

wankapin an American lotus having edible nutlike seeds

wild ash   the American mountain ash
wild date   the Spanish bayonet (or dagger), a desert plant of
southern California
wild leek   either of two perennial herbs
witch hazel   any of various shrubs with slender yellow-petaled
flowers

WHAT KIND OF TALK IS THAT? QUIZ NO. 24
In what subject or field are the following terms
used?

scoring groove	F-coupler
pickup	coupler butt
cutout cock	Ajax Diaphragm
flush handle	humping speed
crabs	SS protection

Answer on page 228.

Squeam Charades

In the parlor game known as charades, some words are easy enough to act out clues for. Other words can be problematical. We're pleased to introduce here a new game called Squeam Charades.

For those willing to venture a game of Squeam Charades, we provide below some particularly challenging words. There are only six rules in Squeam Charades:

1. The game must be played in mixed company only.
2. Players are to be told how many words the mystery term contains and whether it is hyphenated.
3. No "sounds like" clues are permitted.
4. If the mystery term is not guessed within five minutes (these are admittedly mostly uncommon terms), the meaning or definition of the term is to be read to the players; the game then continues.
5. No laughter is permitted.
6. No quitting before the secret term is deduced.

The following list of words is only to get you started. Hundreds of additional terms, of course, may be found elsewhere in this book.

LIST OF WORDS
FOR SQUEAM CHARADES

bissextile day   leap day
climax basket   an oblong basket with rounded ends
ejaculate   to blurt out
intestate   not having provided a will
pismire   an ant
pakapoo   a Chinese lottery
rambong rubber   rubber from the rambong plant
whangee   a walking stick or riding cane of Chinese bamboo
turdiform   like a thrush
lay woman   an unordained woman
masterbatch   a high-concentration mixture of rubber or plastic with a compound
sexdigitism   the state of possessing six fingers or toes
fakir   a Muslim ascetic; a wonder-worker who travels around
fartlek   a regimen of speed training for runners
coxal cavity   a cavity on the lower surface of an anthropod's body
self-tapping screw   a screw that cuts threads in the pieces it secures
coupling rod   a link between two or more cranks, as on a locomotive
smooth aster   a prairie and meadow plant
base horehound   the white dead nettle
sexfoil   a grouping of six leaves or petals
drop-crotching   cutting back a tree's large branches
windbreak   any obstacle to surface winds
donga   a South African ravine

wurstfaggot   a sausage bassoon or rackett, a rare wooden musical instrument

rape oil   an oil, from rapeseed and turnip seed, used for lighting fuel, as a lubricant, and for food

tittup   an affected, prancing way of walking

cunny-thumb   having one's thumb bent behind the second finger with the hand closed

penetralia   secrets, hidden things, or privacy

functor   something that functions

double-tongue   to use the tongue in a particular way in playing a brass musical instrument

screw alley   a passageway housing the screw of a steamer

spermaceti   a waxy solid obtained from the sperm whale

kumquat   a small citrus fruit used for preserves

thrusting screw   an important screw in a cheese press

scum-cock   a valve in a steam boiler

lip-head   a bolt-head projecting on one side only

prickshot   the distance between an archer and the target

Shitrai   a shepherd who is mentioned in the Bible, in 1 Chronicles 27:29

muscular pile   a voltaic battery having animal tissue as elements, used in animal experimentation

flyblow   blowfly larvae; to fill with such maggots; to contaminate

mammock   a shapeless piece

whangdoodle   a mythical bird that grieves continuously

hymeneal   nuptial

dickcissel   the black-throated bunting, a migratory bird

venerean   having to do with Venus or with venery (hunting)

humping track   a railroad yard track for sorting freight cars

hole play   golf in which each hole is scored rather than a counting of total strokes

piloerection   hair standing on end

wangateur   a Louisiana voodoo conjurer

erumpent   bursting through or rising above

cotton teaser   an agricultural machine

crack-loo   a coin-pitching game

organ blower   a motor operating the bellows of an organ

teasehole   a fuel hole in a glass-making furnace

cockchafer   a large European beetle

sext   the monastic prayers of the sixth hour, said at midday

vagitus   the cry of the newborn child

barff   to protect iron or steel, by the Barff-Bower process, with an iron-oxide coating

discharging rod   an electrical discharger

vagina femoris   the sheathlike fascia, or connective tissue, in muscles of the thigh

try cock   one of two valves used to ascertain the water level in a steam boiler

pricker   a horse rider

cundeamor   the cypress vine

jack stud   a middle-height upright framing member in a building

coupling increaser   a type of round pipe fitting

erection wrench   an open-jaw wrench whose handle is tapering or pointed

Bra cheese   a cheese of northwestern Italy

exsuccous   dried up

■   ■   ■   ■   ■   ■   ■   ■   ■

GRAND TOUR OF FORBIDDEN ASIA!

A full three-month itinerary the first-class American way, staying at unforgettable Far Eastern mo-
tels. Talk about Pacific overtures! You will visit:

Asso, Shitadomeno, and Fukahori in Japan
Alabang, Calabugdong, Sexmoan, and Masbate in
   the Philippines
Bangatang Island, Pus Lagoon, Put Put Bay, Kunlip
   Island, Schlangen Island, Pusi Pusi Harbor,
   Pudsey Rock, Foul Bay, and Screw River in
   Papua New Guinea
Pis Island, near Truk
Vuluva in the Solomon Islands
Layang Layang, Gaping, Dong, Endong, Kunkok,
   Titi, Titi Wangsa, and Lingga in Malaysia
Ko Phuket and Bangkok in Thailand
Bangbong, Bangkawang, Ci Kunten, Gunung
   Kunti, Tanjung Cokadu, Poonbaun, Pusipusi,
   Putain, Wanggar, Titigading, Tisispoto Point,
   Pising, Pispis, Fokalik, Meaty Miarang, Aser-
   babber, Labea, Sukadatang, Dong, Sukabares,
   and Gunung Suket in Indonesia
Ban Dong in Laos
Dong Dang and Phuc Yen in Vietnam
Dongdayang, Cuntan, Hungtung, Fucun, Bangtou,

Shitie, Siziwang Qi, Dungfanghang, Wenchang, Pupeng, Longchang, Longdongping, and Dongjug in China

Kuntiyana, Dorka, Suket, Shitab Diara, Poona, Poo, Dong, Cooch Behar, Bangalore, Kanker, Cumbumsouth, Orgi, Hole, Fartia Bhiman, Hardon, Longding, Handibhanga, Hoor, Assa Buttar, and Titrod in India

Sukdeb in Bangladesh

Oralkatcha in the Andaman Islands

Accident Inlet, Dick Creek, Bowelling, Come-by-Chance, Geelong, Mt. Leake, Nukey Bluff, and Humpybong in Australia

Double Cone, Pukemoremore, Pussy Creek, Puketutu, Blow Creek, Fanny Bay, Mount Dick, Dingle Peak, Breast Peak, French Pass, and Whangarei in New Zealand

FOR DETAILS AND BOOKINGS, CONTACT GLOBE-TROTS TRAVEL AGENCY

■   ■   ■   ■   ■   ■   ■   ■   ■

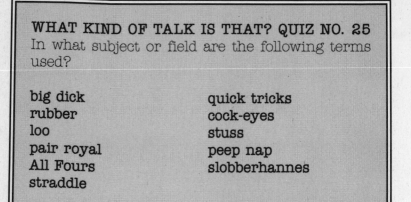

WHAT KIND OF TALK IS THAT? QUIZ NO. 25
In what subject or field are the following terms used?

big dick   quick tricks
rubber   cock-eyes
loo   stuss
pair royal   peep nap
All Fours   slobberhannes
straddle

Answer on page 228.

Sumac College Alumni News

Dear Member of the Class of '78,

Those of you who attended our big 25th class reunion the weekend of May 24–25 know what a huge success it was. If you weren't part of our merry gathering, you'll just have to wait five more years for our next one! In the meantime, though, we'll try to give you a full report here so you know what you missed.

Of our graduating class of 174, 83 members plus quite a few spouses were present for the grand cocktail hour and dinner Saturday night in the alumni banquet room at Crawford Hall.

A number of us " '78 or Bust" class members got a good wet headstart at the cocktail hour, where the mixologists offered everything from a Bosom Caresser to a Greek Buck or Monkey Gland. A lot of B.V.D.'s went down as well. Me, I found a Mamie Taylor and a Dolores to be most tasty. There was also plenty of Bullshot!

Our class was—if you remember that far back!—academically one of the most lustrous in the history of little Sumac College.

Catching up with one and all at our exciting reunion reminded me, once again, how many of us went on to graduate work or into successful careers in the arts.

Here, then, are some items about class members to bring you up to date until we count heads—and graduate degrees!—at our 30th reunion in 1997.

■ ■ ■

Carol Allen, who got her doctorate in psychology, is familiar with the grasping and groping reflex and has published several papers on hemiballism, formication, sex-limited characters, and the jerk nystagmus. (Who is Nystagmus, Carol?)

Ronnie Copes, now an English professor on the West Coast, has been doing scholarly work with a female colleague in diarial style and persuasive tropes, in particular the act of diramens copulatio. He's also keen about something he calls the privie nippe.

Traditional and ethnic "footing it" has been the field of Amy Shapiro, who has worked with the Hora Consort for eight years. She did research in England on "The Milkmaid's Dump" and in California on prominent women who held Cascarone balls. Currently, Amy is focusing on the Danish sextur, Eskimo Angekok, Dutch plugge danse, the turdion, and the Dinka virgin's dance.

Bob McKert only recently read Krapp and got his doctorate in linguistics, with a thesis on generative embedding, class cleavage, and a discovery procedure he calls minimal pair.

Karen Waite is now a therapist specializing in oralism but also has a background in linguistics-phonology. She and Bob were seen going into the ins and outs of faucal plosives, fricatives, and bilabialism. To me it was all pretty guttural!

Mitzi Peaker is a successful graphic artist. She is well informed about the arts of slip trailing and pouncing and also seems to know a great deal about the tusche-washout method. She is inspired mainly by Shinnecock and Coos tribal art.

Jerry Mertz has changed careers, from musician-organist to minister. Until four years ago Jerry taught about organ beaters, portative organs, positive organs, and swell organs at a conservatory. Now he has given up the lure of the fagotto and of labial pipes for a higher calling. At seminary he is doing research on the missionary's position in the Middle Ages and the five ways. Jerry is also an Asser expert and interested in the contemporary Brazilian Boff.

Donald Goldblatt is a passionate erotic poet, with a real feel for feminine endings. His translations from Assamese and Bungku have been published in *Arsis,* where his own verses have been described as Heinesque.

Classmate Myra Woonsock, though not a poet herself, has been teaching classes in the gay science while finishing her doctoral dissertation, "Ectasis and Other Lengthening Problems in Lesbian Odes." Myra and Donald were last overheard chatting about the excitement of the feminine caesura, bucolic diaeresis, and the French liaison.

Ryan Perdido (who is on sabbatical and could not make it to our reunion) is a philosophy professor. At the APA conference last year he read a paper on erotetic approaches, posterioristic positions, and the impersonal proposition. He writes that he is now focusing his research on epistemic privacy.

Melvin Crisp is a social worker. He is interested these days in nerterology and California's peniel missions and helps the socially impotent through the Dorcas Society.

Ken West and Betty Moolick West, who married after graduation from Sumac, are in the Peace Corps in Africa. Betty is fluent in Fang and Ken knows Poke.

If the gods are with any of our graduates, they must be with Max Carling, whose field as an associate professor of classics is ancient Mediterranean religions and deities. He has lectured about the superhuman Dingir of the Sumerians and Mesopotamian worship of the female Mammetum and has published a book about the Egyptians, the goddess Nut, and their reverence for Bubastis and the Tuat region. His forthcoming book, on Roman mythology, will focus on Phorcus, Caca, and Vagitanus.

Jack Puller, the acknowledged "Don Juan" of our class, is now a respected archaeologist and is doing studies in cross-dating and sequence dating.

Miriam Legget, now a political science professor and an active feminist, is working on a monograph on the Non-Intercourse Act. She did her thesis on the Bloody Rump and in her spare time does the black bottom.

Like Karen Waite, Roger Kell is in the field of linguistics. His special field is the phenomenon of cliticizing, but he is also doing research on the anusvara and the performative act.

John Immer wrote his seminary thesis on the anusim. He is now particularly fascinated with Balaam's ass.

Michael Byrne is currently working at the Cleveland Museum of Art, where his interests are Renaissance double cups and French intimism.

Wendell Oliver, now a full professor of anthropology, has investigated homeopathic charms, the Australian Cootchie, the cuntur worshipped by the ancient Peruvians, and the Boobies of Fernando Po.

Jane Elsinore was a flight attendant but became disgusted with recent acts of Aer Lingus. She is now a much-traveled poet, translator of Pissaref, and a past mistress of Yevtushenko, whose lays she loved.

Elliot Watta now has his own antique pottery business, Watta Crock. At the reunion he couldn't stop talking about Eliza Summance's well-formed jugs.

Raymond Teely and his wife Laura (Ferraro) are both professors of musicology. Their lectures on the joys of the bonang, gambang, naker, bass tampons, peckhorn, and quintfaggot are much acclaimed.

Adam Cartmill, on the staff of the India Cultural Bureau in Washington, has written in bureau publications about the Kuntala, the poona pact, and Titu Mir.

Ancient history has been the field of Karen Seinfeld, now an associate professor, who recently gave a series of lectures on Assinarus, Arses, and the Kingdom of the Arsacids. She has no interest in the medieval Arslan but does in the Horites and the Bangs.

Leroy Sanders is now a professor of African history and has written about Kitchener's Dongola, Chief Kok, and Somalia's Mohammed Said Bare.

Connie Nichevsky is a high school music teacher. She has a fertile mind and is always exploring rhythm methods. For her master's thesis she is currently studying the old prick song, pre-minstrel lays, mensuration canons, and virginalists. She has also taken many dumps and explained how people used to dance to them.

James Keene, an archaeologist and Turdetan scholar, will be part of major Middle East expeditions next year to Anafarta Heights in Turkey and Cape Fartak in Yemen.

Debbie Ajax was a theater major and is still a budding actress, finding the life tough. Today, she reports, frustrated actors, who often can't perform, want to see actresses' parts and club owners want you to lie down to do stand-up. But she's keeping her hand in and is always looking for a play with herself as star!

DeWitt Boorman, an ecumenical official for a council headquartered in Seattle, has also written for religious publications about the eighteenth-century American coetus, London bethels, lustration by the impure, and the divines Cock and Hole.

The history of medicine has preoccupied Agnes Welleck since she got her B.S. with a thesis on Coiter. She has lectured on the German Rumph, the Silesian Pansewang, and the Dutch Bra and is now researching the German Boogers.

Joe Bernstein left the field of media consulting to study in Paris and get his doctorate in political science. He is writing his thesis on the well-known Bidet and is well versed in one Fockeday. Joe tells us that certain postgraduate topics were recently assigned and he got the Piles of Marseilles.

Archaeologist Jane Korens writes to us from Athens. She has just finished a book on the French hellenist Cunterius, and now her attention is being focused entirely on the barathrum near the Acropolis. Hope you make it, Jane!

Bob Cratey, who dropped out of Sumac in his junior year, writes that he is into street culture in America and is trying to sell an article on the forgotten joys of grinding organs.

Everett Kord made it to our reunion all the way from Melbourne, where he is getting a doctorate in art history. He is doing his thesis on Guy Head and is looking forward to his orals.

Vanessa Terwilliger, a German major at Sumac, recently won second prize at a Canadian competition among composers. She confesses it has made her a little "cocky," and she is going to do her thesis on either Johann Pansewang or Hugo Schwantzer.

Audrey Klang was doing union work in the West Virginia coal fields but was let go for impairing the morale of miners. At Sumac, Audrey was quite an expert on the period of the Industrial Revolution. She's since been into labor and relations in our time. She constantly misses her old period but feels she is long overdue.

GLOSSARY

Aer Lingus   the Irish commercial airline
Anafarta Heights   a region of Turkey
Angekok   a North Polar dance of the Eskimos and Greenland (also called Tangakoch)
anusim   Spanish Jews forcibly converted to Christianity during the Inquisition
anusvara   in Sanskrit, a continuant nasal sound
Arsacids   successors to Alexander who had a kingdom circa 200 B.C.
Arses   a Persian king (338–336 B.C.)
arsis   in poetry, the stressed part of a metrical foot
Arslan   a Seljuk sultan of the twelfth century
Assamese   a language of India and Bhutan
Asser   a Welsh scholar and bishop of the eighth century
Assinarus   where the Athenians were defeated by Syracuse 415–413 B.C.

Balaam's ass a Biblical ass, in Numbers, which rebuked the prophet Balaam

Bangs an ancient people of Bengal, India

barathrum a pit near the Acropolis in Athens into which live and dead criminals were thrown

bethel a chapel for nonconformists

Bidet, Louis a French chronicler, died 1762

bilabialism making both lips come together to form a consonant, as in *pin* or *mat*

black bottom an American dance popular in the 1920s

Bloody Rump the English parliament coercively created in 1648 by Oliver Cromwell

Boff, Leonardo a Brazilian Franciscan liberation theologian

bonang a Japanese set of gongs made from vases

Boobies of Fernando Po aborigines of Riabba, in the ancient kingdom of Congo

Boogers, Lucas an eighteenth-century German surgeon and author

Bosom Caresser a cocktail with brandy, curaçao, grenadine, and Madeira

Bra, Hendrik van a sixteenth-century Dutch physician and medical writer

Bubastis an Egyptian goddess (also called Bast)

Bullshot a cocktail with vodka and beef bouillon

Bungku a language of Sulawesi (or Celebes)

B.V.D. a cocktail with rum, vermouth, and gin

Caca believed to be a pair of ancient fire divinities (also called Cacus)

Cape Fartek a cape on the Arabian peninsula

Cascarone ball a California ball once held during Carnival around Monterey and Los Angeles (a cascarone was a confetti-filled egg)

class cleavage the occurrence of a linguistic form in more than one form class

cliticizing   an attaching to a word or phrase of a clitic (preliminary or ending form)

Cock, John   an English divine, died 1600

Coiter, Volcher   a sixteenth-century Dutch anatomist

coetus   an eighteenth-century ecclesiastical assembly

Coos   a Native American people of Oregon

Cootchie   the devil, to medicine men of Australia's Dieri tribe

cross-dating   a method of archaeological dating

Cunterius, Jean   a sixteenth-century French scholar of ancient Greece

cuntur   a bird, the condor, worshipped by the ancient Peruvians

diaeresis   a verse division wherein the end of a word is the end of a metrical foot

diarial   like a diary

Dingir   a Sumerian invisible anthropomorphic being considered immortal and superhuman

Dinka virgin's dance   a dance of southern Sudan

diramens copulatio   in rhetoric, a breaking off or interrupting of a conversation

Dolores   a cocktail with both Spanish and cherry brandy and crème de cacao

Dongola   place where the British began their reconquest of the Sudan in 1896

Dorcas Society   a society for supplying the poor with clothing

double cup   a type of decorative standing silver cup of the Renaissance, one of whose twin cups can be inverted and fitted over the other

dump   an old English dance of the sixteenth century; a melancholy song

ectasis   in poetry, the lengthening of a short syllable

embedding   in generative grammar, a process whereby one sentence is embedded within another, as in *The lady who has a purse is in the station.*

epistemic privacy   the content of consciousness accessible only to the person having it

erotetic   pertaining to the procedure of questioning, as in some forms of dialectic

fagotto   a pipe organ stop

Fang   a language of northwest-central Africa

faucal plosive   a stop consonant emitted through the nasal cavity

feminine caesura   in poetry, a caesura after a short or unstressed syllable

feminine ending   in poetry, a final syllable that is unstressed

five ways   Thomas Aquinas's proofs for the existence of God

Fockeday, M.   a French member of the National Convention, 1758–1853

formication   the hallucination that insects are crawling on or under one's skin

French liaison   in French, a common pronunciation linkage

fricative   a type of consonant

gambang   a Japanese xylophone

gay science   poetry

grasping and groping reflex   a reflexive clutching by the fingers or toes when something stimulates the palm or sole

Greek buck   a cocktail with Metaxa brandy and ginger ale

grinding organ   a barrel organ

guttural   sounded in the throat

gyrus fornicatus   the brain's limbic lobe

Head, Guy   an English nineteenth-century painter

Heinesque   in the style of the German poet Heinrich Heine

hemiballism   an involuntary flailing of the limbs on one side of the body

Hole, William   an English divine

homeopathic charms   charms used as folk remedies

Horites   a cave-dwelling Biblical people of the Dead Sea region

impersonal proposition   a proposition having an indeterminate subject

intimism   a genre of French painting favoring scenes from everyday life

jerk nystagmus   regular and repetitive involuntary movements of the eyes

Kok   Adam Kok, a South African Griqua chief with whom the British made a treaty in 1843

Krapp, George   an American writer on linguistics

Kuntala   an area of southern India where the Vakatas extended their power circa A.D. 300–500

labial pipe   a flue (pipe organ) pipe whose tone depends on a lip-like edge

lay   a poem or a song

Lesbian ode   a Horatian ode, simpler in form than the Pindaric ode

lustration   a religious purification ceremony

Maiden's Blush   a cocktail with gin, triple sec or Cointreau, and grenadine

Mamie Taylor   a cocktail with scotch and ginger ale

Mammetum   a Mesopotamian goddess who decided the destinies of man

mensuration canon   in fifteenth- and sixteenth-century music, a fuga, or single part read simultaneously in different mensurations (temporal relationships between note values)

Milkmaid's Dump   a particular sixteenth-century English dance

minimal pair   a so-called discovery procedure used in phonology for determining which sounds belong to the same class or phoneme

Mohammed Said Bare   a Somalian politician of the 1960s

Monkey Gland   a cocktail with gin, Benedictine, and grenadine

naker   a kettledrum

nerterology   learning pertaining to the dead

Non-Intercourse Act   a U.S. embargo (1806) of Great Britain and France

Nut   the Egyptian goddess of the sky

oralism   the teaching of speech to the deaf

organ beater   a medieval organist

Pansewang, Johann   a nineteenth-century Silesian musician and composer

past mistress   a female knowledgeable or proficient in a certain area

peckhorn   a circular kind of althorn sometimes used in place of a French horn (also called mellophone)

peniel mission   a California evangelistic group

performative act   an act following from what is said or done as part of what is being said

Phorcus   an Greek harbor deity, the son of Neptune and father of Medusa

Piles   the name of various governors of Marseilles from the sixteenth through the eighteenth century

Pissaref, Alexander   a nineteenth-century Russian poet

plugge danse   a dance of the Netherlands

Poke   a language of northwest-central Africa

poona pact   a 1931 document that gave lower classes in India more governmental representation

portative organ   a portable, processional organ of the Middle Ages

positive organ   a small chamber organ of the Middle Ages

posterioristic   pertaining to Aristotle's *Posterior Analytics*

pouncing   a process for transferring a design or drawing to paper or another surface, involving pricking and use of a pounce bag

prick song   descant; contrapuntal music; music written down

privie nippe   in rhetoric, the English critic George Puttenham's sixteenth-century term for charientismus: a type of irony that uses an agreeable expression for something disagreeable

quintfaggot   a Tenoroon, or bassoon pitched a fifth above the standard bassoon

Rumph, Georg   a seventeenth-century German physician and naturalist

Schwantzer, Hugo   a nineteenth-century Prussian organist and composer

sequence dating   a technique for dealing with Egyptian predynastic cemeteries

sex-limited character   an inherited trait occurring in only one sex

sextur   a Danish clockwise figure dance for six couples

Shinnecocks   an Algonquian people of Long Island

slip trailing   the application of a clay-water fluid, or slip, to pottery with a syringe device to create linear designs that are slightly raised, as by the Pennsylvania Dutch (also called slip decoration)

Summance, Eliza   a Doulton artist who did floral decorations into the 1920s

swell organ   organ pipes enclosed in a box with side shutters

tampon   a stick having two heads for playing the bass drum

Titu Mir   the leader in 1831 of an uprising in India against Hindu *zamindars*

trope   a verbal figurative device

Tuat   in Egyptian religion, a region far from heaven and from the earth where the dead dwelt

Turdetan   an ancient Iberian people

turdion   a dance like the fifteenth- and sixteenth-century galliard but less spirited

tusche-washout method   a silkscreen and serigraphy technique with a water-miscible black fluid to create effects impossible with a crayon

Vagitanus   the Roman deity who presided over crying children

virginalists   sixteenth- and seventeenth-century composers, notably William Byrd, Thomas Morley, and Orlando Gibbons

wallbanger   a cocktail with vodka or gin and orange juice

Widow's Dream   a cocktail with Benedictine

Yevtushenko, Yevgeny   a contemporary Russian poet

Answers to "What Kind of Talk Is That?"

Index